Amanda Haley will inspire you to look at the Scriptures with new lenses. Combining the best of academic research with her unique brand of humor, topped with a dash of pop culture, she hosts a wild ride through the geography, history, and culture of the Bible. This book will enlighten, inform, and entertain you. Most importantly, you will be equipped with the right tools, resources, and questions to engage biblical study. You will be motivated to look at the Scriptures again from a new perspective. And you might find yourself surprised by what's in there...and even more surprised by what's not.

Heather Zempel, author of *Community Is Messy*
and *Big Change, Small Groups*

Amanda Haley has written an incredibly timely and important work. She bravely navigates the obstacles many of us encounter during faith deconstruction, all while keeping the heart of God the North Star. Blending common sense and scholarly integrity, Amanda has created a seminary-level hermeneutics course in one approachable, holistic, and relatable book.

Dr. Ashley Davis, DMin, author and spiritual director

MARY MAGDALENE NEVER WORE BLUE EYE SHADOW

AMANDA HOPE HALEY

HARVEST HOUSE PUBLISHERS
EUGENE, OREGON

Cover design and illustration by Kristi Smith, Juicebox Designs

Mary Magdalene Never Wore Blue Eye Shadow
Copyright© 2019 by Amanda Hope Haley
Published by Harvest House Publishers
Eugene, Oregon 97408
www.harvesthousepublishers.com

ISBN 978-0-7369-7512-4 (pbk)
ISBN 978-0-7369-7513-1 (eBook)

Library of Congress Cataloging-in-Publication Data

Names: Haley, Amanda Hope, author.
Title: Mary Magdalene never wore blue eye shadow / Amanda Hope Haley.
Description: Eugene : Harvest House Publishers, 2019.
Identifiers: LCCN 2019004528 (print) | LCCN 2019022236 (ebook) | ISBN
    9780736975124 (pbk.)
Subjects: LCSH: Bible--Hermeneutics. | Common fallacies--Miscellanea. |
    Bible--Criticism, interpretation, etc.
Classification: LCC BS476 .H2355 2019 (print) | LCC BS476 (ebook) | DDC
    220.601--dc23
LC record available at https://lccn.loc.gov/2019004528
LC ebook record available at https://lccn.loc.gov/2019022236

Printed in the United States of America

19 20 21 22 23 24 25 26 27 / BP-RD / 10 9 8 7 6 5 4 3 2 1

For Rachel and Jennifer

Your honest questions
revealed to me how humans' traditions
can sometimes obscure the beauty, power,
and truth of God's Scripture.

CONTENTS

INTRODUCTION

S o why didn't the other disciples respect Mary Magdalene's authority in this text?" asked the teaching fellow in my Apocryphal Jesus class. We were analyzing the Gospel of Mary, a second-century writing that exalts Mary Magdalene as Jesus' beloved apostle and is not part of the Bible for several reasons—most obviously that more of the manuscript is damaged than is legible.

There were about ten students there, and we were all seated around a big table in a windowless room. It was a graduate course at the Divinity School, but undergraduate students were allowed to take it. Across from me sat DeWitt, a Harvard senior who (as I remember him) always wore a popped-collar pink polo and a smirk.

I volunteered the first answer: "Maybe it's because she was a prostitute?"

DeWitt could not control his laughter. "Mary Magdalene was *not* a prostitute. How did you make it to grad school without knowing that?"

The TF tried to smooth things over by calmly explaining to me that the Bible does not claim Mary was a prostitute. That was a traditional, not scriptural, belief that had been introduced by Pope Gregory I in the sixth century.[1] In my defense, it was 2003 and *The*

DaVinci Code was not yet the worldwide phenomenon that has since made this fact common knowledge.

I don't remember too much more about the not-in-the-Bible-for-good-reasons texts we studied that semester. But as tends to happen in life, that embarrassing mistake taught me a more important lesson: we must examine Scripture itself so we know the differences between what God said in the Bible and what people say about the Bible.

When I told my mother what had happened, she was livid. She recalled that when she had dressed up as Mary Magdalene for a children's Easter play at her church, her mother had smothered her face in makeup because—as everyone knew—Mary Magdalene was a prostitute. (And apparently first-century prostitutes wore a lot of blue eye shadow.) I was at least the third generation of my family who wholeheartedly believed the Bible said something that it does not.

So how did I make it to grad school without knowing that? I grew up in the Bible Belt and attended church Sunday mornings, Sunday evenings, and Wednesday nights—as did my mother and her mother before her. We "knew" the Bible as well as anyone else in our churches; we also knew our churches' teachings and traditions. But we didn't know how to differentiate between them. The traditions had been taught to us as if they were the inspired Word of God.

I can't imagine there's some Sunday school teachers' convention where everyone is trained in how to use felt boards, serve animal crackers, and indoctrinate children. No, when laypeople and sometimes even the ordained mistakenly teach Christian traditions or denominational beliefs as if they are scriptural truths, they do so because they believe what they are saying. This is why James says, "teachers will be held to a higher standard" (James 3:1, THE VOICE): teachers must know how to study the Bible for what God says and not just recite to students what they have been taught.

Traditions get elevated to doctrines—and eventually honored as equal to Scripture—when people fill in details they think the Bible has left out. In the case of Mary Magdalene, Pope Gregory was trying to give a name to the woman who washed Jesus' feet in Luke 7:36-50. He chose Mary Magdalene simply because hers is the next woman's name in the text (Luke 8:2). Because Pope Gregory was the authority for the Catholic Church at the time, no one questioned his teaching. When the people heard that Mary Magdalene was the adulteress of Luke 7, they took the rumor and ran with it. And as all rumors do, it grew until Mary became the archetypal blue-eye-shadow-wearing prostitute I saw on Sunday school felt boards. Academic and armchair scholars alike may debate whether or not Gregory's intentions were insidious and misogynistic, but the fact is he filled something in where he thought God had left something out. This was false teaching.

But it wasn't all Gregory's fault. For fourteen hundred years, a chunk of Christianity—myself included—didn't bother to fact-check him or any of our other teachers. When Grandma, Mama, and I read Luke 7, we imagined Mary Magdalene as the woman washing Jesus' feet simply because we'd always been told she was there. We trusted our teachers more than we scrutinized Scripture, and we unwittingly enabled others to do the same. We three knew what we believed but not why we believed it. We'd learned Bible stories instead of study methods.

We need to stop treating the Bible as a big collection of fairy tales or a sixty-six-chapter rule book and start studying it as the culturally, literarily, theologically, and historically unique Scripture that it is. This is a challenge that often requires us to reconsider our own long-held traditional beliefs. Reading the Bible in its original context instead of from our own contexts may teach us that what we thought was truth is legend. Admitting we are wrong or ignorant is humbling, but it is the necessary beginning of a dynamic faith that is sensitive to God's Word and properly reflects Him to the world.

When Christians cling to traditional beliefs more strongly than to scriptural facts, we confuse the gospel for ourselves and others. What should be a glorious message of grace and love that draws people to Jesus is too often perceived as a rigorous list of dos and don'ts that brands Christians as hypocritical and hateful. The Bible needs to speak on its own, free from the doctrines and traditions we have created around it, to show humanity who God is and how He has worked.

When we are growing in our understandings of and relationships with God, we can recognize false teachings such as Pope Gregory's fill-in-the-blank theology and the noncanonical Gospel of Mary. While it is true that the manuscript is badly deteriorated and incomplete, the document's physical condition is not the primary reason it is not part of the Bible. It contradicts canonized Scripture, claiming that Jesus reserved special teaching for Mary's ears only, and that He loved Mary (not John) the most of His disciples.[2] Both Gregory's denigration of Mary Magdalene and the noncanonical gospel's exaltation of her obscure the disciple's true character as revealed by God in Scripture. *The DaVinci Code* does the same. All three prove why it's better to get biblical history from the Bible itself rather than from tradition or, worse, from popular fiction.

Studying Scripture begins with knowing what the Bible is and what it isn't, what it says and what it doesn't say. This book aims to give you that foundation and encourages you to seek God in His own words rather than accept a version of Him that has been altered by tradition. Why? Because God has revealed Himself in Scripture, not in creeds or hymns or books like this one, no matter how righteous they may be.

Chapter 1

GOD'S LIBRARY
IN ONE BOOK

Every year just before Easter, my hometown's churches volunteer for a twenty-four-hour, four-day-long Bible Reading Marathon. They've done this for as long as I can remember, and for the same number of years, the church I grew up in has seemingly been assigned a graveyard shift and the "worst" books for such an event: 1 and 2 Chronicles. Just imagine standing outside at 3:00 in the morning reading aloud, "Now Benjamin begot Bela his firstborn, Ashbel the second, Aharah the third, Nohah the fourth, and Rapha the fifth. The sons of Bela were Addar, Gera, Abihud, Abishua, Naaman, Ahoah, Gera, Shephuphan, and Huram" (1 Chronicles 8:1-5), and so on for the fifteen to thirty minutes you are at the podium. It does, indeed, feel like a marathon.

Passages such as that give the Chronicles their reputations as the most boring books of the Bible. The long genealogies, tongue-twisting names, and hypnotic repetition are occasionally broken up by narrative stories, but even those read as sanitized copies of Samuel and Kings. Chronicles seems to offer nothing to the casual Bible reader, so why on earth is it in there? For that matter, how did any of the books make it into the Bible?

From Many Scrolls to One Book

Thanks to my father, I've learned a lot about books. Not in the reading-is-my-hobby kind of way (although that's true too), but in a books-are-business way. Before he retired, Daddy worked for a book distributor. He spent his days figuring out how to get books from the company's warehouses and print-on-demand facilities to bookstores and households as efficiently as possible. What mattered to his job was not the intellectual material he was moving all over the world, but the physical material. Over the last two decades, no one has had a better view of how technology has changed one of the oldest industries in the world.

We take for granted the accessibility of books. Today, thanks to on-demand publishing, it is possible to print a hardbound Bible on the same machine that just spit out a copy of *War and Peace*. Neither production would take more than a minute, and the resulting books would look similar: hard cover, thick spine, paper pages, and black ink. And with the growing popularity of free shipping deals offered by various retailers, you no longer have to go to a brick-and-mortar store to get one of those hot-off-the-press books. Daddy could have had it on your doorstep in two days or less.

The density and uniformity of almost any book feels powerful in a reader's hand. We assume the pages between the cloth-covered cardboard contain words that have been written, translated, edited, and designed to perfection just for our pleasure or edification. For no book is this truer than the Bible, but what we can hold in one hand today is a poor reflection of the ancient library it actually represents.

Materials

Writing a book takes effort. It begins with an idea and then requires the author to sit down for hundreds of hours to record those thoughts. As a so-called Xennial who was taught to write research papers using index cards and note cards but now bangs her ideas directly into a virtual Word document, I know that writing is easier and far less time-consuming than it was just twenty years ago. I no longer have to write everything in longhand on a legal pad, edit on paper, and then type out a perfected copy on a word processor. I don't need Wite-Out for corrections, and I don't waste money on paper and ink supplies.

Go back not twenty but two or three thousand years from those typewriter days, and the effort required to write a "book" began with making—not buying—materials. The men (yes, *men*—we'll get to that) who took the time to record the words of Scripture sacrificed not only their time but sometimes their animals. Although pieces of Scripture can be found all over the Near East painted onto buildings and pottery, pressed into clay and wax, and even engraved on metal and wood, the more-or-less complete copies of books of the Bible primarily survive on parchment and papyrus.

WHAT HAPPENED TO BC AND AD?

The first thing a biblical archaeology student learns on her first day of a theology class is dating. Three things to keep in mind:

1. There was no Year 0, so each millennium (and century and decade) begins on a 1. That means we should have been partying "like it was 1999" on December 31, 2000, because the twenty-first century didn't actually start until January 1, 2001.

2. The years prior to nonexistent Year 0 count backward. Even theologians need to understand the mathematics they struggled to learn in high school.

3. The designations BC ("before Christ") and AD (*anno Domini*, "in the year of our Lord") have been replaced by BCE ("before the common era") and CE ("common era") in scholarship. When I first learned about this change, I thought the world was trying to get rid of Christ. While there might be some truth to that statement, I agree on the whole that the new date designations are better for everyone. The most obvious reason is that most archaeologists in Israel are Jewish, so BC doesn't make a whole lot of sense to them. But the more important reason is that Jesus probably wasn't born AD 1; 4 BC (or maybe even a bit earlier) is a better fit for His birthday considering historic, literary, and archaeological facts. It is less confusing if Jesus was born "before the common era" than "before Christ"; that second designation would instigate all sorts of theological conundrums![1]

Ostraca

An issue for many biblical scholars is the lateness of the first complete version of the Hebrew Bible (Protestants' Old Testament). It was preserved in two distinct versions: a Hebrew version (as one would expect) called the Masoretic Text and a Greek translation called the Septuagint. The first complete Hebrew Bible is called the Leningrad Codex; it was made in 1008 CE. The first complete Greek Bible (both Old and New Testaments) is called the Codex Sinaiticus; it was made around 350 CE.

This is not to say that the Hebrew Bible was simply dreamt up thousands of years after some of its events. Fragments of Scripture are literally all over the ancient Near East—often in ancient trash heaps—dating as early as the tenth century BCE.[2] These fragments are called *ostracon* or *ostraca* (plural); they are often broken pieces of pottery with ink lettering. Scribes would apparently write on whatever material was available, no matter how cumbersome.

Arguably the oldest record of biblical Scripture was found on a broken piece of pottery in 2008 during an excavation of the biblical city called Sha'arayim or Shaaraim (mentioned in Joshua 15:36; 1 Samuel 17:52; and 1 Chronicles 4:31). This was a border city between Philistia and Judah during the reign of David in the eleventh century BCE. The pottery's text roughly coincides with 1 Samuel 8, where the last judge of Israel, Samuel, describes what will happen to the people when the nation becomes a monarchy.

Around the year 1000 BCE, when that piece of pottery was inscribed with Samuel's warning against the Israelite tribes requesting a unifying king, the words were not yet Scripture. They were news. Or maybe a journal. Someone wrote down Samuel's words because he wanted to remember and thought others should be able to read what he had heard come from the prophet's mouth. Of course, those words never traveled outside of the city from which they were written, indicating the one major problem with writing on broken pottery (or stone or wood or clay): it isn't very portable. The ancient world needed to develop writing mediums that could travel and could hold more than a few dozen words.

Parchment

The first thing that comes to mind when I hear the word *parchment* is a diploma. Today diplomas are printed on parchment paper, as are other important documents such as marriage licenses, land deeds, commendations, and even resumes. Parchment paper is usually heavy, tan, and textured, imitating its leather forerunner. But have you ever heard someone call a diploma a *sheepskin*? Have you ever wondered why the traditional image of a diploma is a ribbon-tied scroll although none of us store them that way today? All diplomas were inked onto leather sheepskin—not paper—up until the 1950s.[3]

The leather-making process hasn't changed much in the last five thousand years. Animal skins were cleaned of dirt, blood, hair, fat, and flesh and then cured in water-based solutions containing salt or even urine. The skins were then rinsed before they were soaked in another solution containing plant extracts. The wet, tanned leather was then stretched to dry.[4] The whole process took months.

Any leather, no matter how thick or what color, could be inked by scribes and rolled into scrolls. Entire libraries of leather scrolls, most famously the Dead Sea Scrolls from Qumran, exist today thanks to the durability of leather.

Parchment is essentially an extremely thin, tanned leather. Whereas standard leather could be heavy and was readily available to all, parchment was lightweight and costly. Beginning in the fourth century CE, it became the ideal medium for Scripture recording because it could be carried easily from one community to another and could withstand being rolled and unrolled—no ribbon necessary—almost countless times as it was copied and read.

Papyrus

Even before their first dynasty was founded in 3100 BCE, the Egyptians were making papyrus sheets. It had advantages over the leather scrolls—most obviously its light weight—but it was delicate, perishable, and expensive. It was also produced exclusively by the state. No one was allowed to collect reeds for their own use;

everything belonged to the pharaoh, and he dictated who made how much papyrus and for what purposes.

Tall papyrus reeds naturally filled the Nile River's delta marshlands. Workers would harvest the plant first from those wild deposits and later from cultivated fields. The damp stalks would be sliced into pieces so the pith could be removed from the center and pounded flat. Two pieces would then be pounded together, with one pith running horizontally and the other vertically, until they merged into one inseparable and quite strong sheet of papyrus. Sheets could then be placed alongside others and pounded together into sheets of any length. Once dried in the sun, the sheets could be rolled up with the vertical pith to the outside and the horizontal pith on the inside.[5]

The Egyptians used papyrus primarily for their court and religious documents; it was not an ancient schoolboy's notebook paper. They widely exported it during the Greek and Roman Empires, but it was not used in the ancient Near East until the first century BCE. This is fortunate, as papyrus rarely survived outside of Egypt's uniquely ideal climate of dry-but-salty air and consistently warm temperatures. Egypt has just enough humidity and salinity to keep the scrolls supple but not so much that the papyrus would mold. Had more Israelite and Jewish scribes used papyrus instead of parchment, we would have even fewer artifacts to learn from today.

Technique

Ancient scribes never could have imagined the print-on-demand machines publishers enjoy today. For them, the great technological wonder was ink. By mixing charcoal and oil or red ocher and gum, scribes could record any letter instantly—when compared to the old chisel-and-stone method—and in color!

For hundreds of years, scholars have debated when exactly the first Scriptures were recorded. Considering all discovered media—from walls and pottery to jewelry and scrolls—the (arguably) oldest biblical text archaeologists have found is inscribed on a tiny silver scroll that someone would have worn on a necklace around 700 BCE.[6] It is roughly the text of Numbers 6:24-26:

> The LORD bless you and keep you;
> The LORD make His face to shine upon you,
> And be gracious to you;
> The LORD lift up His countenance upon you,
> And give you peace.

Have you ever been to a fair and watched someone writing on grains of rice and selling pendants in which to wear them? The microscopic words supposedly bring luck to the wearer. Consider this modern curiosity (itself with ancient Eastern roots) an equivalent to the ancient and highly symbolic silver scroll amulet. In a largely illiterate ancient society, someone took the time to write a scriptural blessing on a costly piece of silver that (he assumed) would never again be read once finished. Written words were meaningful—maybe even magical.

Until scribes began diligently recording the Hebrew Scriptures onto parchment scrolls for use in the temple and later in synagogues and churches around the world, God's words were known through long-told stories and memorized prayers passed down within families from generation to generation. Why did it take so long for Scripture to proliferate? Because texts required skill, time, and money to create. And someone who could contribute all three was more likely to be employed by the state than religion.

Consider the scribes mentioned in the Hebrew Bible: each one serves in a king's administration, be it Israel's or a foreign power's.

David's and Solomon's often nameless scribes pop up all over Samuel and Kings. Ezra, who famously rebuilds Jerusalem after the exile, did so at the command of the Persian king Artaxerxes, whom he served as the court's Jewish attaché. Even Baruch, who served as the prophet Jeremiah's personal scribe, came from a noble family of royal scribes.[7] Quite obviously, it was political service that "paid," and not religious service.

The royal exclusivity of the written word diminished during the Hellenistic period (332 BCE–70 CE), after Alexander the Great had conquered the ancient Near East. As his Greek traditions were imposed across the soon-to-be Roman Empire, nationalism arose among the Jews and the dissemination of Scripture became important to retaining their culture as Greek values began transforming Jerusalem physically and socially. Scribes began copying scrolls in earnest for the temple's use. The young men who had learned how to write the Hebrew alphabet began copying the as-yet uncanonized biblical books letter by letter. If one of them made a mistake—no matter how close he was to completing the scroll—it would be buried and never read.

Around the same time, the codex—folded pages nested within other folded pages and stitched together, not unlike this book you are holding—supplanted the scroll as Most Likely to Be Portable in the literary world. The story goes that Ptolemy V of Egypt, in a desperate attempt to keep his library at Alexandria the fount of knowledge in the ancient world, banned the export of papyrus. This was what motivated Eumenes II of Pergamum to invent *parchment*. Ptolemy's plan backfired as the durability, flexibility, longevity, and reusability of parchment flooded the new "book" market. Codices were often smaller and lighter than their scroll counterparts. Their pages could be inked on both sides, and readers could more quickly flip to the sections they wanted to read. The publishing world never looked back!

CHAPTER AND VERSE

Once the Bible had been canonized and scribes were generally copying the same content from one codex into another, the disparate books and letters that make up Scripture came together in one book that we would mostly recognize today. But once all those bits and pieces were together, the volume of information in one place proved cumbersome and made study challenging. So the church decided to break it back apart.

In 1227 CE, a professor at the University of Paris and a future archbishop of Canterbury, Stephen Langton, divided the Latin version of the Christian Bible into chapters. His work was considered so logical that his chapter divisions were adopted not only by the Catholic Church, but by Jewish rabbis as well. That he produced such sensible and enduring work is not surprising, as Langton had also been key to the writing and passage of the Magna Carta in 1225, which ushered in modern Western democracy.[8]

About three hundred years later, a French printer named Robert Estienne gave us the verse divisions. Have you ever been reading a passage of Scripture and thought, *that is divided in a strange place*? Maybe you've wondered as I have, *why does the story of Adam and Eve begin in Genesis 2:4 and not Genesis 2:1?* The old joke goes that Estienne made his verse divisions while riding his horse from Paris to Lyon, so any apparently stray verse number must be the result of the horse stumbling and the pen slipping. This story, though humorous, is the product of a mistranslation from Latin into French and then into English. In a letter to his son in 1551, Estienne claimed he did the work *inter equidantum*, which can be literally translated "on horseback," but more likely meant "while traveling."[9] No horses were involved in the division of our Bible, but this story is a great example of how inaccurate translations can foster false belief.

Printing Press

Those newfangled "books" could be quickly disseminated thanks to Johannes Gutenberg's invention of the printing press in 1439. His development of durable type molds—not unlike the backward-facing letters you see on the arms of old typewriters—enabled him to set the text of one page of a Bible one time and then print multiple copies of it in ink on parchment. This invention would prove critical to the dissemination of Protestant ideas (and Bibles) in the following decades and centuries. By 1825, printing presses would be making three distinct Bibles—Jewish, Catholic, and Protestant—each containing different books from the others.

Seventy-five years later, many of those Protestant Bibles got makeovers with the introduction of red-letter editions. Typesetters and printers now had the awesome responsibility of choosing which words (in the Old and New Testaments) belonged to the Christ and carefully inking them with red instead of black.[10] Although I doubt inventor Louis Klopsch had the ancient scribes and their handmade black and red inks in mind when he chose red as the secondary color, he unwittingly paid homage to the scribes' aching backs, strained eyes, and cramped hands that preceded modern book printers and distributors who now need only forty-eight hours to get lightweight, perfectly inked copies to your doorstep.

In spite of the volume of ink and quantity of paper I just wasted explaining what the Bible is physically, none of that really matters. Your personal copy of the Bible might be paperback or leather bound. If you use an e-reader, then your Bible does not even exist in a concrete sense. A Bible's physical material has plenty of monetary but zero spiritual value. The spiritual value is found in the words themselves, not the ink or pixels that form them.

Languages

The Bible I most frequently study is printed in my native language: English. The New King James Version's Scripture is in English, its footnotes are in English, and its study tools are in English. The linguistic accessibility makes it easy to forget that the books inside were not written in 1981 (when the translation was first published) by English speakers for English speakers.

When I read the New King James Version, I am studying a *translation* of Scripture—not the Scripture itself. And what I learn from the text and notes printed between the covers is totally dependent on the people who translated it from the original languages for my postmodern-living, Western-thinking, English-reading brain.

I am not Scripture's original audience. First, the English language as we speak it today was unknown even at the time of the printing press. Second, the last words of the Hebrew Bible (in the book of Malachi) were probably recorded around 300 BCE. That's a twenty-three-hundred-year gap between biblical authors and current readers, if you're counting. So translators have to consider linguistic *and* cultural differences between writer and reader.

Hebrew

With a few exceptions, the original words of the Old Testament were written in Hebrew. The earliest manuscripts are continual strings of consonants, written from right to left. Early readers could look at just those consonants and understand the text based on oral traditions *without the benefit of vowels, punctuation, or even spaces.*

Let me state that again: wthtthbnftfvwlspncttnrvnspcs Makes the modern Oxford comma debate seem silly, doesn't it?

Consider how important vowels can be to determining the tense of an English verb. *SWM*, depending on the vowel added, could mean "swim" (present tense), "swam" (past tense), or "swum" (past perfect tense). Hebrew vowels have an even greater impact on a word's meaning; they can determine not only verb tense, number, and gender, but also the part of speech. In Hebrew, a vowel can change a word from a verb to a noun or adjective or direct object. Their importance cannot be overstated.

When the Masoretes started copying the Hebrew Bible in earnest during the sixth century CE—giving us our earliest complete copies of the Hebrew Bible in existence—they decided to add vowels to their transcriptions. Why? Because much of Hebrew's grammar is transmitted through its vowels, rendering punctuation unnecessary. They knew from tradition what vowels were intended between the consonants, and they wanted to make reading Scripture easier for future generations. The thing is, vowels don't really exist in written Hebrew, not as we think about them. Vowels are not characters; they are little lines and dots—glorified accent marks, really—written above, below, or within the consonants. Adding the vowel marks made the scribes themselves the first Bible translators; their work made the text readable for anyone who was literate in Hebrew, and not just the rabbis.

Greek

The New Testament was almost entirely written in Koine ("common") Greek during the first century. This language was a bit of an amalgamation of all Greek dialects across the Roman Empire. What was written on parchment did not necessarily match what one would say. Consider formal English and southern American English.

I regularly use *y'all* when I am speaking to more than one person, but I would write *you* or *all of you* in formal publications because that would be understood by any English reader, regardless of his or her proximity to the Mason-Dixon Line.

Biblical Greek is closer to the English language than biblical Hebrew in that it is written from left to right (instead of right to left) and vowels are actual letters. But its grammar is still quite different from English grammar, and its alphabet is unique. Whereas English uses individual words for different parts of speech, Greek tacks prefixes and suffixes onto nouns to make very long words we would translate as phrases. Consider the translations of some Greek words with which you are familiar:

> anonymous: "without a name" (*an* – "without" + *onoma* "name")
>
> gymnastic: "relating to physical exercise," (*gymnos* "naked" + – *ikos* "pertaining to")
>
> Philadelphia: "loving brother" (*philos* "loving" + *a* – "together in" + *delphys* "womb")

Does the etymology of that second word surprise you? It proves a great point: even when one language completely adopts a word, such as *gymnastic*, from another language, its meaning can change. Throughout the Roman Empire, young men would gather at a gymnasium for exercise and education. When sports were practiced and performed, the men would be naked. Clearly the "naked" denotation of *gymnastic* fell away in America, where we (thankfully) play basketball and balance on beams fully clothed.

Aramaic

One other language creeps up occasionally in the Bible. It

accounts for about half a dozen chapters of the Hebrew Bible and is quoted in the New Testament roughly eight times. Why mention such a rarely used language? Because its sparsity in the Bible does not reflect its actual importance in the ancient Near East. Aramaic was the international language for communication and literature in the region between 600 BCE and 700 CE. This means that Aramaic was spoken almost the entire time the biblical scrolls and, later, codices were being recorded and copied.

Aramaic is a cognate language of Hebrew, meaning they both came from the same source (as Spanish and French both come from Latin). In fact, the Hebrew alphabet is wrongly named; Hebrew uses the Aramaic alphabet. Their grammars and much of their vocabularies are similar, to the delight of every biblical theology student.

Aramaic was on Jesus' lips and on the lips of almost everyone He encountered. Mel Gibson got that right in his 2004 film, *The Passion of the Christ*, even if we can't precisely reconstruct the first-century pronunciation. It was spoken by Jews, Christians, and Samaritans until Arabic took over in the region around 1200 CE. This is why most Aramaic in the New Testament is a direct quotation of someone's words. The books and letters themselves may have been written in the imperial language, but Jesus' last words were too important to risk anything being lost in the translation from Aramaic into biblical Greek:

> "Eloi, Eloi, lama sabachthani?" which is translated, "My God, My God, why have You forsaken Me?" (Mark 15:34).

Dates

Obviously there is no such thing as a word-for-word translation of the Bible because Hebrew, Greek, and Aramaic do not follow the same grammatical rules as English, and societies' customs influence words' meanings in ways other communities cannot understand.

Let's go one step further: there is no such thing as a word-for-word translation from biblical Hebrew to modern Hebrew or biblical Greek to modern Greek because location is not the only influencer of language. Time is a factor as well.

Scholars continue to debate exactly when the Bible was written, but it is generally accepted that the Old Testament was inked onto parchment between 1000 and 200 BCE and the New Testament between 50 and 95 CE. Consider all that happened during this millennium of writing:

- the united monarchy divided into Northern Israel and Southern Israel in 930 BCE,
- the Assyrians conquered Northern Israel in 722 BCE,
- the so-called Lost Tribes of Israel were then exiled throughout the Assyrian Empire and beyond,
- the Babylonians conquered Southern Israel (also known as Judah) in 586 BCE,
- many Judahites were exiled throughout the Babylonian Empire from 586 to 538 BCE,
- the Persians helped build a new Jerusalem between 538 and 515 BCE,
- the Romans conquered the Persians and the new Jerusalem in 63 BCE,
- the Romans began persecuting Christians in 64 CE, and
- the Romans razed the new Jerusalem in 70 CE.

Any one of those events would change a person's perspective of the world and could alter his or her language.

Have you heard the saying "Loose lips might sink ships"? That was the American government's way of reminding its citizens not to share state secrets with Axis enemies in World War II.* It's one of the ways my mother taught me that gossip is dangerous. But without World War II and that iconic slogan, how would English speakers interpret the words, "Loose lips might sink ships"? Would we think *lips* was a euphemism for something else, such as round, mouth-shaped floats? In that case, the slogan would mean that unpreparedness (deflated innertubes) leads to destruction (drowning). Plausible? Yes. Correct? No. Clearly history—time and events—influences language, meaning, and the writers who wield the pens.

Authors

When I was growing up, my favorite book series was Ann M. Martin's The Baby-Sitters Club. Each book is the adventure of one of the ten babysitters in the "club" as she (or he, in the case of one male babysitter named Logan) faces adolescence and cares for the often-rambunctious children who live in the neighborhood. The series has overarching themes of personal growth and community understanding, but each book is told in first person by just one of the ten babysitters who handwrites parts of some chapters and has a singular ambition that is usually achieved by the end of her book.

Each of the babysitters has a stereotypical characteristic: Kristy is athletic and in control, Mary Anne is shy and bookish, Claudia is artistic and outgoing, and Stacey is New York City cool. It is easy to accept any one of the ten protagonists as your avatar throughout the series. I was a classic Mary Anne...who wanted to be a Stacey.

---

* Ironically, the famous poster was produced by Seagrams Distillers Corporation, the producers of one of the world's "lip looseners": Canadian whiskey.

Twenty-five years later, I am still a Mary Anne...who actually enjoys being a Mary Anne. I'd rather be secretary than vice president. I'd rather my clothes be smart than runway-ready.

Like the books of The Baby-Sitters Club, each book of the Bible has a distinct author with a particular point of view and personal history. Themes of each biblical book may be similar, but the stories told are unique to their settings and characters.

Moses is credited with originating the Torah (the books of Genesis, Exodus, Leviticus, Numbers, and Deuteronomy, known as the *law*). We tend to think that means he sat down and wrote the first version of the Israelites' history in Hebrew on an ancient leather scroll, but it is far more likely that the Bible is crediting Moses as the author of the Torah's oral tradition. Much as John F. Kennedy is the credited author of the Pulitzer Prize-winning book *Profiles in Courage*—but he, as many other politicians have done, allegedly used a ghostwriter who "did a first draft of most chapters" and "helped choose the words of many of its sentences"[11]—Moses was the speaker of God's oral tradition, which would inspire Spirit-led scribes to write down the words that officially formed the sacred Torah as we know it today.

Kings David and Solomon may also have been the inspirations for and oral originators of the Psalms and Proverbs, which are credited to them, but based on textual analysis of the dialect in which those Scriptures are written, it is more likely that they, too, had ghostwriters who recorded the words we know today. Those writers would have been scribes who lived centuries after the great kings had died and who themselves may have experienced atrocities such as foreign conquest and exile that influenced their vocabularies.

Writers were influenced by the international politics around them. Before Israel was decimated by foreign powers, the scribes—who were likely employed by the Israelite government to preserve

Israel's political and religious history—seem to have been quite honest in their recording of Israel's exploits. The good, bad, and ugly all appear on the page. Take Kings David and Solomon, as described in the books of Samuel and Kings: they are men "after His own heart" (1 Samuel 13:14), "wise" (1 Kings 5:7), and loved by Israel and God (1 Samuel 18:16; 2 Samuel 12:24). But David was a murderer (2 Samuel 11:15), and Solomon worshipped other gods (1 Kings 11:4). Before the Babylonian destruction of Jerusalem and her temple in 586 BCE, scribes seem to have recorded a rather unbiased history.

Now compare the stories of David and Solomon in the books of Samuel and Kings to the stories in 1 and 2 Chronicles, which were recorded by scribes after Judah's exile in the Babylonian Empire. Chronicles does not mention David's affair with Bathsheba or the bad behavior of his oldest sons Amnon and Absalom. It ignores Solomon's worship of foreign gods. Two or three centuries after Samuel and Kings were recorded, these so-called Chroniclers were inspired to describe a history of David and Solomon that was pure and righteous—one that might then inspire the Jews who were returning to Jerusalem from their generation of Babylonian exile and rebuilding a city they had never seen themselves.

By implying that much of the Bible was "ghostwritten," do not think that I in any way am nullifying the sanctity and inspiration of the books of the Bible as God's Word. Quite the opposite. As a former ghostwriter myself, I have been involved in projects where I was the one recording the "jots and tittles" of someone else's inspired work so their ideas could make it from the computer screen through the printing press and into the hands of readers. I like to think that God used the talents He had gifted to me to complete those projects, regardless of whose name was credited on the books' covers. And I know that I thoroughly enjoyed every book in The Baby-Sitters

Club series, no matter who was the fictional babysitter narrating or who was the real-life ghostwriter recording those words.[12]

Formats

A major difference between The Baby-Sitters Club and the Bible (because there are so few differences, right?), is that each book of the fictional series follows the same format. It is a prose story told from a first-person perspective. But the books of the Bible vary in their literary forms; there is poetry, prose, and correspondence—and sometimes all three appear together in one book. A book of the Bible may have one author or many. The author(s) may speak in first or third person. The unique characteristics of each book means that the Bible is not a series but a collection. An *anthology*, to be more precise.

First came poetry.

What were your favorite children's stories when you were learning to read? It had been about three decades since I'd given much thought to Dr. Seuss and the Berenstain Bears, but since my two-year-old preliterate niece found my stash of old books, I've been reading them regularly. When I'm reading *to* Harper, she requests the Berenstain Bears because the pictures are pretty. When I'm reading *with* Harper, she goes straight for *The Foot Book* and *Hop on Pop* because she can "read" them herself. Yes, she is starting to recognize the letters on the page, but what she calls *reading* is actually reciting. She remembers a lot of the words because they rhyme.

There is nothing particularly remarkable about Harper's tendency to remember words that rhyme or follow a simple tune, even at the young age of two. When she sings to me, "Jesus loves me, this I know...," she is simultaneously learning and teaching an important truth that has been passed down to her through song. She is participating in oral tradition, the forerunner of literature. Before people could read tablets or scrolls or books, they learned their history and theology and culture through lyric poetry. This was true for all ancient societies, including Israel.

Based on their form, vocabulary, and grammar, the oldest passages included in the Bible—the Song of the Sea (Exodus 15:1-18) and the Song of Deborah (Judges 5)—are lyric poetry. The scribes who recorded the Scriptures included these poetic songs as is within the prose narratives of Exodus and Judges presumably because everyone already knew the words by heart. This is not surprising, considering the likely low rate of literacy among the ancient Israelites. People would have composed these songs for two reasons: first, to remind future generations how God protects His people, and second, to memorize the events of the Red Sea crossing and the defeat of Canaan's General Sisera.

About one-third of the Hebrew Bible is written in poetry. You find it sprinkled throughout the narrative books (such as Genesis and Judges), but it dominates Psalms, Proverbs, Job, and many of the books of the prophets. Each poem tends to have an obvious internal structure, and parallelism is common; both of these characteristics aid in memorization. Sadly, the rhymes and rhythms and sometimes even the imagery inherent to the original Hebrew tend to get lost during English translation.

Psalms

Because no ancient equivalents of sheet music have been discovered, it is easy to forget that the Psalms formed Israel's original hymnbook. These poems would have been sung or chanted by the priests and Levites in the temple as a way of honoring God or requesting His help. Topics range from praise of God's goodness to sorrow over enemy threats. Some psalms honor the anointing of a new king, while others are road-trip music for annual Jerusalem pilgrimages. Just about every topic is covered.

The songwriters used tons of imagery—most commonly pastoral imagery, which is an idealized depiction of life as lived by farmers and shepherds in the country and away from the chaos of the city. Let's consider an English translation of the first four verses of everyone's favorite, Psalm 23:

> The LORD is my shepherd;
> I shall not want.
> He makes me to lie down in green pastures;
> He leads me beside the still waters.
> He restores my soul;
> He leads me in the paths of righteousness
> For His name's sake.
>
> Yea, though I walk through the valley of the shadow of
> death,
> I will fear no evil;
> For You are with me;
> Your rod and Your staff, they comfort me.

The songwriter assumed everyone who read this would have a connection to the pastoral life. If they weren't shepherds themselves, then they knew people who were. They understood how shepherds cared for sheep by using the same stick to discipline them as they used to protect them from predators. *Shepherd* and *sheep* are the perfect metaphors for God and humanity.

A mnemonic device that tends to get lost in translation, as do rhyming Hebrew words, is the acrostic. I'm sure you are familiar with these. Every letter starting a word or phrase lines up vertically to spell something else. Some people like to turn *B-I-B-L-E* into an acrostic stating, "basic instructions before leaving earth." That is silly and incorrect (we'll discuss it more in chapter 7), but you see what I'm describing.

In the Hebrew Bible, acrostics don't spell words but are made from the descending letters of the alphabet. When we were translating Psalm 119 and other acrostics like it for The Voice Bible, translators and editors all attempted to retain the artistic nature of the poems by translating each line to start with a subsequent letter of the English alphabet, but it was impossible. We could either keep the ABC format (which itself was wrong because the Hebrew alphabet is closer to ABG when transliterated), or we could translate the words correctly and ignore the original structure of the poem.

In most translations of the Bible, it is easy to see the compromise in Psalm 119. Each stanza is "titled" with the transliterated letter of the Hebrew alphabet that begins it in the original language. (So if you ever want to learn the Hebrew letters and are really bored during a sermon, just whip out Psalm 119 and start memorizing! Aleph-Beth-Gimel-etc.)

Song of Songs

During one of the required-of-all-students theology classes in undergrad, I sat beside an art major who was perpetually bored. Most people in that class would have rather not been there; whenever the professor asked a question he'd pause, see no raised hands, and then look for a pity answer from one of the few theology majors there whom he knew was actually listening. (Of course if you were one of the theology majors, you *had* to do the homework and listen in class because there was no hiding from him.)

One day we were discussing Song of Songs—something the professor thought would surely get everyone's attention—but most people seemed to be lost in the figurative language. It did manage to engage my neighbor. He made his first contribution to the class:

a cartoon of the Shulamite woman as described by her future husband in Song of Songs 4:1-5. She had

- a bird peeking out of each eye socket,
- horned goats tangled in her hair,
- a family of naked sheep in place of each tooth,
- skinny red lines for lips,
- pomegranate halves stuck on the sides of her head,
- a thick, loooooooong Corinthian column as a neck, and
- a baby Bambi lying among Stargazer lilies where each breast should be.

Song of Songs is full of similes and metaphors that absolutely do not translate to today's readers. Even if there could be a perfect word-for-word translation, the book would make no sense because you need to know what birds, pomegranates, and gazelles represented to ancient Israel. To understand imagery, you have to understand the community that produced it.

So what did the writer mean when he described this woman so bizarrely? Let's consider what each image represented in ancient Israel.

- "You have dove's eyes behind your veil" (v. 4:1). Like a dove hiding among the rocks or in a tree, she looks to be innocent, maybe a bit anxious, and very alert.
- "Your hair is like a flock of goats, / Going down Mount Gilead" (v. 4:1). Imagine watching this from a distance: the animals in varying colors of brown would move as a fluid unit back and forth among the rocks as they descended. It would look a lot like those shampoo ads

in which women with long brown hair toss their waves side-to-side in slow motion.

- "Your teeth are like a flock of shorn sheep...and none is barren among them" (v. 4:2). This one isn't quite as hard to interpret as it initially seems. Her teeth are clean—that's pretty obvious—but how could they "bear twins" or be "barren"? I think this woman had ancient orthodontia. Her teeth are perfectly shaped. They match each other, and none are missing.

- "Your lips are like a strand of scarlet" (v. 4:3). I don't think the emphasis here is on the "strand" but on the "scarlet." Her lips are red, full of blood, alluring.

- "Your temples...are like a piece of pomegranate" (v. 4:3). We could fall victim to a poor translation here. It would be better rendered "your cheekbones." Her cheeks may be high and firm, or a lovely rosy pink. Or all of the above.

- "Your neck is like the tower of David..." (v. 4:4). She is strong and regal. She cannot be easily conquered.

- "Your two breasts are like two fawns / Twins of a gazelle / Which feed among the lilies" (v. 4:5). Obviously there is no resemblance in shape between fawns and breasts, so I think the man is describing the impression that her figure inspires. Her breasts are young and playful. The lilies (or lotuses) they stand among are common ancient representatives of fertility because the blossoms resemble a womb.

When her description is read with knowledge of the society

that produced the poem and the images they commonly used, the woman is obviously lovely, young, fertile, and alluring.

We still enjoy poetry today. Isn't it easier to memorize a Bible verse when it is set to a tune? As a child I loved the "Fruits of the Spirit" song with coconuts and watermelons and silly faces; as an adult I appreciate the fact that it taught me Galatians 5:22: "The fruit of the Spirit is love, joy, peace, longsuffering, kindness, goodness, faithfulness, gentleness, self-control." Tastes change, but human brains will always memorize the same way.

Then came prose.

I don't think I've ever heard a preacher say, "the Bible is plain ole great literature." But it is. In school we study similes and metaphors, foreshadowing and hyperbole, euphemisms and parables, and so many other literary devices that make good writing good. We pick apart and write essays about Leo Tolstoy (less so Ann M. Martin, sadly), and we try to learn the tricks of good writers so we can become better writers ourselves—or at least understand what the good writers are trying to convey.

Every one of those literary devices—and so many more—are found and well-used in the Bible. Of course a lot of the art of biblical prose gets lost in translation, literally, because certain images such as a camel going "through the eye of a needle" (Matthew 19:24) don't make sense to our twenty-first-century, English-speaking brains. We want to gloss over metaphors we don't understand instead of taking the time to learn the historical context of the image and then translate its purpose to our lives.

Our high school literature teachers would not have let us get away with ignoring what we could not understand in fictional prose. Did you ever read Nathaniel Hawthorne's *The Scarlet Letter*? In brief, it is the story of a seventeenth-century woman who has an affair with a Puritan minister, the Massachusetts Bay colonists who shun her for it, and her eventual redemption. Throughout much of the novel, she wears a scarlet-colored *A* on her chest that, as Hawthorne himself explains, "was her passport into regions where other women dared not tread." It is a symbol of sin, shame, and (more literally) adultery. But by the end of the story she has made amends and become a sort of confidante to the next generation of Puritan women in her community who wrestle with their own "shame, despair, and solitude." The *A* comes to represent so much more than *adultery*; Hester is regarded more as an *angel* at her death.[13]

If we are willing to spend weeks studying a novel, no matter how classic it may be, then we should hold ourselves to the same or higher standard when it comes to Scripture interpretation. There is no point in reading *The Scarlet Letter* if the reader gives no thought to the symbolism and the Puritan traditions that inform it. Likewise, we can miss the purpose of God's words if we don't investigate the images, ironies, and allegories He inspired the scribes to record so many centuries ago.

Then came letters the apostles composed.

Although we don't know who committed most of the books of the Hebrew Bible to parchment, we do know the authorship of almost all the New Testament books. Aside from the Gospels (which were written by their namesakes), the Acts of the Apostles (which is really just part 2 of Luke), and the Revelation of John (which is in a class all by itself); the New Testament is a collection of letters written by Paul, James, Peter, John, and Jude to Gentile and Jewish Christians across the ancient Near East and Mediterranean. The Epistle to the Hebrews remains the only book with a mysterious provenance, but its themes suggest the writer was a disciple of Paul.

The writing of formal letters with instructive purposes was

common in the Roman Empire. Such elegant letters had their own name: *epistles*. The New Testament letters, though each was addressed to a particular audience when written, would have been passed from church to church and even city to city as the young Christian movement standardized its beliefs in Jesus and practices of worship. Paul and the other writers were teaching their friends God's promises through Jesus and how the Christian communities should differentiate their lives from the surrounding non-Christians'. Whereas the artistic poetry and prose of the rest of the Bible sometimes require discernment for understanding, the New Testament epistles are refreshingly direct. They tell people what to do and what not to do, what to believe and what not to believe.

In the absence of a distinct Christian canon during the first centuries, the apostles' letters were the early converts' only Scriptures outside of the Hebrew Bible Jesus Himself had studied.

Unifying Canons

When you read the word *canon*, please notice there is only one *n* in the middle. The selection and standardization of holy Scriptures did not involve iron war machines (although the theologians undoubtedly had heated debates with one another).

Most world religions have found that canonization is necessary at some point. Without it Jews, Christians, Muslims, and Buddhists alike would be unable to differentiate their religion's truths from false teachings. A *canon*, by definition, is a measuring rod. In a religious context, it is a set of standards developed by leaders to evaluate writings pertaining to their religion. How those writings developed are central to why they are chosen to join a canon. Writings may be evaluated based on authorship, date, style, content, and harmony with other already-accepted Scriptures.

As the new Christian religion matured and expanded, its leaders realized they needed a cohesive set of Scriptures on which they all agreed and from which they would teach. That canon has come down to us, centuries later, as the Bible. This is divided into two parts or *testaments*. The Old Testament roughly coincides with what the Jews call the Hebrew Bible, and the New Testament contains first-century writings sacred only to Christians.

The Hebrew Bible

The Hebrew Bible has three parts: Torah (the first five books, all attributed to Moses), Prophets, and Writings. Each of these three sections became part of the closed Jewish canon at a different time in history. Honoring the development of the Hebrew Bible as a whole, Jewish Bibles orient the books according to those three grand divisions (whereas Christian Bibles order the same books more or less chronologically).

The Torah, which is the Law, was the first section of the Hebrew Bible to be accepted as God's Word. Scholars disagree on exactly when that happened, but it must have been before Ezra read it aloud to the Jews returning from Persia to help rebuild Jerusalem:

> Now all the people gathered together as one man in the open square that was in front of the Water Gate; and they told Ezra the scribe to bring the Book of the Law of Moses, which the LORD had commanded Israel. So Ezra the priest brought the Law before the assembly of men and women and all who could hear with understanding on the first day of the seventh month. Then he read from it in the open square that was in front of the Water Gate from morning until midday, before the men and women and those who could understand; and the ears of all the people were attentive to the Book of the Law (Nehemiah 8:1-3).

These events described by Nehemiah happened in 445 BCE, so the Torah had to have been officially adopted as the Jews' law book prior to that date.

The canonization of the Prophetic books also can be dated by their proximity to the Persian exile. Jewish tradition holds that all prophecy stopped when Alexander the Great conquered the Persians in 332 BCE. Assuming that is correct, the Prophets had to be closed prior to that date. If the section had remained uncanonized after 332, then there might have been prophets of God speaking to Israel about the coming Roman Empire. Also, Chronicles and Daniel would be counted among the Prophets; instead they are canonized with the Writings. Linguistics further support the idea that the Prophets were closed at the turn of the fourth century BCE. Had the Prophets been working after Alexander's conquest, Greek words would probably have worked their way into the biblical text.

Of the three parts of the Hebrew Bible, the canonization of the Writings is hardest to date. It has long been believed that the Writings were canonized at the rabbinic Council of Jamnia around 90 CE. However, all that can be confidently assumed is that the Writings were canonized by the time of the Bar-Kokhba Revolt (132–135 CE), when the Jews tried to push the Romans out of Judaea and rule themselves.[14]

The Christian Bible

Not until 1546 CE, when the Protestant Reformation was spreading across Europe, did the Roman Catholic Church authoritatively declare which books belonged in the Bible and which did not. At the Council of Trent, church leaders evaluated the arguments of five early Christian theologians regarding the books they each proposed for the New Testament. Jerome's fourth-century Latin Vulgate version of the Bible was selected as the church's official canon.

The New Testament part of that canon was also accepted by

Protestant churches, but Jerome's translation includes eleven inter-testamental books. These so-called deuterocanonical books fill in the time gap between the Old and New Testaments. While Protestants and Jews do not view them as authoritative, several of the books (especially the Maccabees) are helpful records. They have literary and historical, if not spiritual, value.[15]

I used to attempt to read the Bible cover-to-cover once every year. There was a chart in the back of my Bible to help me do that, so I assumed that was what everyone was supposed to do. I managed to accomplish it only once, and I was disappointed to discover that achieving my goal did not do much to help me better understand God. In fact, the exercise bred frustration and boredom, and its completion tempted me to pride in my own imagined success.

A Bible Reading Marathon, whether executed over four days in the public square or during a calendar year in a private space, isn't the best way to study Scripture and meet God. The best way to read the Bible is to study it not as a giant novel but as the anthology that it actually is. It is a collection of the works of multiple authors, over many centuries, writing in different languages with different media. Each book developed independently and has a unique perspective of God, and so it deserves to be read as its own unit with an understanding of how it came to exist. Then the books should be considered in concert with one another, because together all sixty-six are the complete Word of God.

So why did God choose to reveal Himself to us in such an indirect way? Wouldn't it be easier and faster for Him to host a semiannual press conference to tell us all what He wants us to know than for us to have spent millennia mistaking and misteaching His words probably more often than we understand them?

Since He created us, God's desire has been to walk alongside us in His perfect garden. He wants us to have relationships with Him, and as we know from interacting with one another, relationships form only after people have spent time learning one another's histories and goals and have chosen to live life together. If God had chosen to dictate to us, then we would be His slaves and not His children. He wants us to invest time learning about Him, and for some reason only He fully knows, the best way to meet Him is to read every book in His library—the boring genealogies, the seemingly repetitive histories, the confusing laws, the beautiful poetry, and even the mysterious prophecies.

It takes a long time to read and study every single book in a library; in fact, it is an assignment that can't really be completed in any person's lifetime. God hasn't asked us to finish this getting-to-know-You marathon in world-record time. Instead, He wants us to spend our lives cultivating the relationship as we walk with Him in the garden, not run toward a finish line.

Questions for Discussion and Reflection

1. Scripture has a long history of physical development from oral traditions through papyrus and parchment to the print- and e-books we read today. Why do you think God has chosen time and again to update the media that preserve His sacred Word?

2. From Moses in the wilderness to modern missionaries worldwide, God has inspired thousands of people in the recording and translating of the Bible. Why do you think God involved so many humans in the transmission of His perfect Word?

3. The Bible contains examples of almost every form and genre of literature. Why do you think God's Word showcases His creativity instead of speaking simple rules and regulations?

Chapter 2

DON'T IGNORE
YOUR TEXTBOOKS

I have a dear old friend who is an astronomy professor. We first met about ten years ago when he started attending a church small group of twelve that my husband David and I hosted every other Friday evening in our home. I would serve a homemade dessert and coffee, and we all would sit around the kitchen table eating and talking about Scripture for about two hours. Most people were gone by 10:00, but Nathan often lingered. In those late hours when the small group had become a tiny one, Nathan and I would frequently interrupt each other, trying to turn the conversation back to the other person's field of study because we each preferred the other's day job.

I am an astronomy lover. When I was a child, my daddy and I would spend brisk fall and warm summer evenings staring at the night sky. First he taught me to recognize Orion, the Big Bear, the Southern Cross (or what little we could see of it from Nashville), and the Summer Triangle; then he taught me the names of the stars in those constellations. He'd point at the sky and ask me to name one dot of light, and he loved trying to trip me up by pointing at a planet—or satellite—instead of a star.

Whenever I lost my bid to control the post-small group conversation with Nathan and David, it often turned to the Bible's depiction of natural phenomena. What does God's Word say about the creation of the universe, the age of the planet, and the evolution of humanity? Was there really a worldwide flood? How did Moses part the Red Sea? Will the Left Behind books become reality?

Questions such as these were particularly difficult for Nathan, who held a PhD in physics but was raised in a very conservative Protestant tradition whose members prided themselves on "reading the Bible literally." Every Sunday as he was growing up, his faith was unnecessarily put at odds with his common sense. His childhood church had wanted him to choose between God and science, but he felt that was an unnecessary and false choice. We agreed.

Let Carl Sagan Teach You About the Cosmos

Most Gen-X science enthusiasts have fond memories of Carl Sagan and his beautiful and informative series, *Cosmos: A Personal Voyage*, that aired on public television in 1980. (Nathan, David, and I are all Xennials—born on the cusp of the Gen-X and Millennial generations—who watched *Cosmos* on elementary school filmstrip projectors, or if we were lucky, roll-into-the-classroom tube televisions with VCRs.) The thirteen-episode series explained many natural phenomena from a purely scientific point of view, including the origin of life, the workings of the universe, humans' impact on the planet, and the possibility of extraterrestrial life. Sagan's work was so popular that it has been reinvented and updated for a new generation with host Neil DeGrasse Tyson as *Cosmos: A Spacetime Odyssey*.[1]

Now, I don't watch these shows because of the worldviews of the hosts; truthfully, I watch in spite of them. Neither man shares my faith or my values—Tyson even mocks Christianity rather openly—but their scientific insights have actually broadened my belief in God. They believe that the more we understand about the workings of the universe, the more obvious it is that God does not exist. I counter that the more we understand science, the more obvious it is that this universe is not some happy accident full of coincidences and happenstance. The more complex and beautiful the cosmos, the more of God I see in it.

Weeks before he died of a rare blood cancer on December 20, 1996, Carl Sagan wrote to a no-longer-atheist (but not Christian either) colleague, criticizing him for suggesting there just might be one Creator God and an afterlife. Martin Gardner's response was perfect: "I not only think there are no proofs of God or an afterlife, I think you have all the best arguments. Indeed, I've never read anything in any of your books with which I would disagree. Where we differ is over whether the leap of faith can be justified in spite of a total lack of evidence."[2]

I think it is hard for intellectually brilliant people to make leaps of faith regardless of their vocations. Highly analytical minds want to take everything apart, see all the pieces, and understand them. There is a certain pride that comes with total understanding, and a simultaneous fear of the unknown. That combination of pride and fear too often leads great scholars to belittle people of faith as weak, wrong, silly, and useless.

But it works the other way too. Too many Christians take pride in their extrascriptural beliefs, fear science they interpret as contradicting the Bible, and belittle scholars as weak, wrong, silly, and useless. No one trying to learn about creation is any of those things. Christians should engage with scientific discovery, be awed by God's work, and pray that everyone will see Him in the "atoms as massive as suns, and universes smaller than atoms."[3] Sadly, Sagan never did.

Creation of the Cosmos

The Bible gives us two accounts of creation. God stoically commands everything into existence from afar in Genesis 1:1–2:3. (There's one of those strange chapter and verse divisions we mentioned in chapter 1!) God gets His hands dirty in His garden in Genesis 2:4–3:24. Let's discuss that first version, as it describes the creation of our world *and* the rest of the universe:

> In the beginning God created the heavens and the earth. The earth was without form, and void; and darkness was on the face of the deep. And the Spirit of God was hovering over the face of the waters.
>
> Then God said, "Let there be light"; and there was light. And God saw the light, that it was good; and God divided the light from the darkness. God called the light Day, and the darkness He called Night. So the evening and the morning were the first day...
>
> Then God said, "Let there be lights in the firmament of the heavens to divide the day from the night; and let them be for signs and seasons, and for days and years; and let them be for lights in the firmament of the heavens to give light on the earth"; and it was so. Then God made two great lights: the greater light to rule the day, and the lesser light to rule the night. He made the stars also. God set them in the firmament of the heavens to give light on the earth, and to rule over the day and over the night, and to divide the light from the darkness. And God saw that it was good. So the evening and the morning were the fourth day (Genesis 1:1-5,14-19).

When you read the entire passage, you learn that it takes God six "days" to create the universe and everything in it. That one English word—*day*—is why so many scientists and Christians cannot agree.

You didn't have to be a fan of CBS's late comedy series *The Big Bang Theory* to know that is the name of the accepted scientific understanding of how the universe came into existence. It goes something like this:

> In the beginning there was nothing. No space, no time, no heat, no light. Then—literally out of nowhere—there was a "singularity." It was infinitely tiny, denser than dense, and hotter than hot. It started expanding and cooling, and light was born. We now live inside the singularity, which we call the *universe*.
>
> Stars, planets, and satellites started popping up about 200 million years later. Bits of matter from the singularity stuck to each other, created gravity fields, and started sucking in other bits of matter to form solid spheres. As those spheres grew and their gravity fields neared each other, all the stars, planets, and satellites started pushing and pulling against each other until they oriented themselves into galaxies and solar systems.

According to scientists, it took 13.8 billion years to get from nowhere to here. That's a lot longer than six days! And the universe is still expanding and forming.[4]

Whenever I hear the Big Bang Theory, I think, *That sounds a lot like what Genesis describes*: Light popped out of nothing. Big stars came together, and then planets and moons did the same. The big stars started pulling the smaller planets and moons into their gravitational fields. Earth settled in near the sun, and the moon settled in next to earth. That summary fits both the biblical and scientific arguments, if you ignore the time part.

So how long did all this take—was it 13.8 billion years or six days? Let's examine exactly what the Bible says.

WHAT IS *TRANSLITERATION?*

Languages such as Hebrew, Greek, Arabic, and Russian use a different alphabet than English does. This, naturally, makes the languages more difficult to translate and to explain.

Say I wanted to understand a Spanish word. If it were written down, I could recognize the letters and pronounce it to some degree. Just speaking or hearing the word might even give me a clue as to its meaning. The Spanish word English translates to "god" is *dios*. Based on the letters alone, I could guess the meaning because we have words such as *deity* in English that are obviously related to the Spanish *dios*.

But in Hebrew, *God* is אֱלֹהִים. Would you have any idea how to pronounce that? Without forming a deep and loving relationship with a Hebrew textbook, there is no way you could. Those don't even look like letters to the English reader. So how do we make אֱלֹהִים pronounceable for the non-Hebrew speaker? We transliterate.

Each character of the Hebrew alphabet sounds like a character in the English alphabet. So instead of writing אֱלֹהִים, we write *Elohim*, substituting our letters for Hebrew's sounds. This helps the non-Hebrew readers "hear" the language as they read.

The Hebrew word usually translated as "day" is *yom*. Ignoring any context, that is an accurate translation. But that word can also mean an undefined "period of time." *Yom* could be translated as "year," "period," or even just "time." The meaning of *yom* is influenced by the exact words, Hebrew grammar, and narrative actions surrounding its use in the text. Let's look at two examples where *yom* clearly does not mean "day":

> If a man sells a house in a walled city, then he may redeem it within a whole year after it is sold; within a full year [*yom*] he may redeem it. But if it is not redeemed within the space of a full year, then the house in the walled city shall belong permanently to him who bought it, throughout his generations. It shall not be released in the Jubilee (Leviticus 25:29-30).

Leviticus 25 is an absolutely thrilling chapter full of laws about all kinds of property and what can and cannot be done with it every seven years. Knowing the context of the passage as a whole, and seeing that there is no mention of literal "days" anywhere in it—years are the only unit of time—then it is obvious that *yom* means "year" here. If it meant a literal twenty-four-hour day, then verse 29 would be contradicting itself on either side of the comma.

> And the period [*yom*] that he reigned over Israel was forty years; seven years he reigned in Hebron, and thirty-three years he reigned in Jerusalem (1 Chronicles 29:27).

This is part of King David's obituary summarizing the length and locations of his reign over Israel. What the NKJV translates as "period" and the KJV translates as "time" in that verse is a plural form of *yom*. They are right to avoid translating the Hebrew into the very literal English "and the days" because the Hebrew does not literally mean "and the days were forty years"—because that doesn't make much sense—but "and the period of time was forty years."

In Genesis 1:1–2:3, *yom* is used fourteen times, and every single time most English translations use the word "day." Technically this is correct: *yom* is "day," but not always in the sense of "one rotation around the earth's axis." So what does *yom* mean in this chapter— "twenty-four hours" or "a period of time"? Based on the location and purpose of this passage, the answer might be *both*.

Genesis 1 is a sort of formal introduction to the anthology that is the Bible. It is an epic, poetic, awe-inspiring description of the beginning of everything that highlights God's godliness. He speaks, and the cosmos is created in a time before time itself existed. Genesis 1 has a second purpose that is far less exciting and much more practical: it explains why a week has seven literal twenty-four-hour-long days. As the rest of the Bible describes, and as civilizations have since put into practice, men and women work six days each week and rest on the seventh. Why? Because God Himself figuratively kept "the Sabbath holy" (Exodus 20:8-11) long before His laws had been given to the Hebrews. These two simultaneous functions of Genesis 1—one poetic and one practical—make it impossible to choose between *yom*-as-time and *yom*-as-twenty-four-hours because both are correct.

It truly doesn't matter whether or not *yom* means "twenty-four hours" in Genesis 1 because creation is no less amazing if it took 13.8 billion years instead of seven days to get us here. God is epically powerful and wonderfully loving. He could have done anything with that so-called singularity, but He chose to make us out of nothing. When readers of Genesis 1 miss the point of the passage because they are more interested in discrediting science with literature or vice versa, they just might miss how much God loves us. After all, these are just numbers; choosing the right combination isn't the key to entering heaven.

Age of the Planet

So if *yom* doesn't necessarily mean "day"—and there are many passages in the Bible where it does not—then how could we even begin to use the Bible to figure the age of the earth? If it didn't work for the universe, then it isn't going to work for the planet either.

One of my friend Nathan's major stumbling blocks was the so-called Young Earth Theory. This states that earth is not yet ten thousand years old, based on the dates and ages of people mentioned throughout the Hebrew Bible.[5] Tossing aside for the moment all the conflicting dates within Scripture itself and the number of biblical scrolls and codices that might have a 9 written where a 7 should be (we will cover all of that in chapter 6), this is still an impractical theory because, once again, it ignores literary devices such as euphemisms and exaggeration and relies on a flawed-but-literal English translation.

Yom isn't the only Hebrew word with about a million possible meanings. Add to it the phrase *arbaiym shaneh*, which the New King James Version consistently translates as "forty years." Does the Bible say "forty years"? Yes. But does it mean "forty years"? Not usually. That is a euphemism for "a generation," so unless a new set of Gen-Xers or Millennials popped up every forty years—to the day—then there is no way to count the exact years of the Bible, let alone use them to figure out the age of the planet.

If he were here today, Carl Sagan would tell us the earth is 4.5 billion years old. During his series *Cosmos*, he introduced the world to his "cosmic calendar," which visualized the age of the universe in proportion to twelve months. The Big Bang happened the first second of January 1, and all human history is in the last ten seconds of December 31. On his calendar, the earth was formed September 6.[6] A Young Earth equivalent of that calendar would have the universe, the earth, and civilization all born in the first five minutes of January 1.

The main nontheological reason Young Earth theorists discredit the scientific theories is that they distrust radiocarbon dating. This method of determining the age of organic material is commonly used by geologists and archaeologists all over the world. It is imperfect, but it isn't totally useless, as Young Earthers sometimes claim. Beta Analytic, a major testing lab, describes radiocarbon dating this way:

> Radiocarbon, or carbon 14, is an isotope of the element carbon that is unstable and weakly radioactive. The stable isotopes are carbon 12 and carbon 13.
>
> Carbon 14 is continually being formed in the upper atmosphere by the effect of cosmic ray neutrons on nitrogen 14 atoms. It is rapidly oxidized in air to form carbon dioxide and enters the global carbon cycle.
>
> Plants and animals assimilate carbon 14 from carbon dioxide throughout their lifetimes. When they die, they stop exchanging carbon with the biosphere and their carbon 14 content then starts to decrease at a rate determined by the law of radioactive decay.
>
> Radiocarbon dating is essentially a method designed to measure residual radioactivity. By knowing how much carbon 14 is left in a sample, the age of the organism when it died can be known.[7]

Many environmental factors can change how fast or slow an organism breaks down carbon 14, different methods of measurement may yield different results, and different labs have higher success rates than others. You are never going to be able to say, "That fossilized frog died on June 1, 307 BCE," but you can narrow down the time of his demise to a century or less. On a 4.5-billion-year-old earth, that is rather impressive.

So how long do geologists say it took for earth to take shape and become inhabitable? Remember, it started out as formless matter that spun and spun with gravity into a sphere about 4.5 billion years ago. After one hundred million years of that physical formation, the atmosphere (which Genesis calls "the firmament," incidentally) settled around the globe, allowing the temperature to stabilize, gases to balance, water to condensate, and algae to grow when the earth was about 2.1 billion years old. It would be another 500 million years before the atmosphere resembled what we breathe today. During that transition, water that had covered everything began peeling back into oceans and lakes and rivers, leaving behind dry land. Grass could now make its debut.[8]

WHAT IS A *FIRMAMENT?*

Then God said, "Let there be a firmament in the midst of the waters, and let it divide the waters from the waters." Thus God made the firmament, and divided the waters which were under the firmament from the waters which were above the firmament; and it was so (Genesis 1:6-7).

That one part of creation never made much sense to me. I would picture some sort of cyclone in the middle of the ocean or maybe Cecil B. DeMille–style Red Sea water walls. I had no clue what God was doing here.

In an undergraduate class about Asian religions, of all places, the verses were finally explained to me. The ancient Easterners viewed themselves as living in the middle of water because they thought the blue sky was blue water, like the sea. The *firmament*

was what we might call the horizon line of the atmosphere—
something invisible that dammed the water above their heads,
leaving the dry air space in between. Of course that dam would
sometimes spring a leak, causing some of the sky-water to fall
to earth as rain.

As with the creation of the universe, if you ignore the time ele-
ment, Genesis and science aren't that different in their descriptions
of events:

> Then God said, "Let the waters under the heavens be
> gathered together into one place, and let the dry land
> appear"; and it was so. And God called the dry land
> Earth, and the gathering together of the waters He called
> Seas. And God saw that it was good.
>
> Then God said, "Let the earth bring forth grass, the herb
> that yields seed, and the fruit tree that yields fruit accord-
> ing to its kind, whose seed is in itself, on the earth"; and it
> was so. And the earth brought forth grass, the herb that
> yields seed according to its kind, and the tree that yields
> fruit, whose seed is in itself according to its kind. And
> God saw that it was good. So the evening and the morn-
> ing were the third day (Genesis 1:9-13).

I am newly impressed every time I reread just how much Genesis got right about the creation of earth. Of all cultures' creation stories, the Hebrew Bible's version is the most plausible and the only
one with a chance of being supported by science. And it is millennia older than the science that agrees with it.

Contrast Genesis 1 with one Chinese creation myth: the god
P'an Ku was born from an egg whose yolk and white were actually
yin and yang. He made the world by hand, and when he died, his

flesh and bones became soil and rocks. Then the fleas on his corpse developed into humanity.[9] Ick-factor aside, we aren't going to be finding out humans evolved from fleas anytime soon.

Origins of Natural Phenomena

Some people refer to Genesis's Creation account as an *etiology*. That's no more than a big, fancy word for "origin story."

I have an origin story. As I was growing up, people would ask me, "Where did your red hair come from?" because both my parents are brunette and, at that time, there were no other natural redheads in my extended family. I would always answer, "From Daddy's mustache." That very short story did two things: it solved what was a great mystery for young me, and it revealed scientific truth. I now understand that my red hair came from the hidden, recessive red-hair genes my parents gave me at conception, but before I could understand biology and genetics, my "origin story" truthfully identified my father as one source of my hair color.

If you've ever watched one of those DC or Marvel Comics movies that never seem to leave theaters, then "origin story" is a term with which you are familiar. Why can Spiderman shoot webs from his wrists? He was bitten by a radioactive spider. Why can Superman fly? He is a refugee from another planet. Why is Wonder Woman immortal? Her parents are Greek gods.

Origin stories are not unique to superheroes or even fiction. The Bible has tons of origin stories, especially in the book of Genesis, that answered the questions of *why* and *how* in nonscientific but still factual ways that ancient minds could understand. Obviously the Creation account is an etiology for everything in existence: Genesis explains the origins of everything before humans understood the science, and these stories are true. But written within that creation account is another origin story: the snake. Genesis 3:1-15 explains why snakes slither on the ground instead of walking as other land creatures do.

> So the LORD God said to the serpent:
> "Because you have done this,
> You are cursed more than all cattle,
> And more than every beast of the field;
> On your belly you shall go,
> And you shall eat dust
> All the days of your life.
> And I will put enmity
> Between you and the woman,
> And between your seed and her Seed;
> He shall bruise your head,
> And you shall bruise His heel"
> (Genesis 3:14-15).

The snake was cursed to such a lowly existence (pun intended) because it convinced Eve to eat fruit from the Tree of Knowledge of Good and Evil.

As you can see, etiologies tend to be little stories unto themselves. They may be included in longer narratives and are often central to the plot of a bigger story, but they can also stand on their own. Possibly the most famous (and obvious) etiology in the Bible is the origin of the rainbow. God told Noah after the flood waters had receded,

> This is the sign of the covenant which I make between
> Me and you, and every living creature that is with you,
> for perpetual generations: I set My rainbow in the cloud,
> and it shall be for the sign of the covenant between Me
> and the earth. It shall be, when I bring a cloud over the
> earth, that the rainbow shall be seen in the cloud; and I
> will remember My covenant which is between Me and

you and every living creature of all flesh; the waters shall
never again become a flood to destroy all flesh. The rainbow shall be in the cloud, and I will look on it to remember the everlasting covenant between God and every
living creature of all flesh that is on the earth (Genesis 9:12-16).

Thanks to science, we know how rainbows form. Water drop-
lets, such as those that remain in the clouds after a rain, are natural
prisms. As light passes through them, it is bent and then split into
all the colors that our eyes usually can't see.

We understand the science behind rainbows, but ancient scribes
weren't privy to information about refracted light. They knew that
rainbows appear after a storm when the first light breaks through
storm clouds. They saw the arches up in the sky, on the firmament
between God's heaven and man's earth. They knew God put the
rainbow in the sky to reassure us that He would never again flood
the earth, in the same way I knew Daddy was the source of my hair.
Both the story and the science are correct.

Of course, not all etiologies are ancient complements to modern science. They can also explain social and cultural practices. Read
Genesis's account of the Tower of Babel:

> Now the whole earth had one language and one speech.
> And it came to pass, as they journeyed from the east,
> that they found a plain in the land of Shinar, and they
> dwelt there. Then they said to one another, "Come, let
> us make bricks and bake them thoroughly." They had
> brick for stone, and they had asphalt for mortar. And
> they said, "Come, let us build ourselves a city, and a
> tower whose top is in the heavens; let us make a name
> for ourselves, lest we be scattered abroad over the face of
> the whole earth."

But the LORD came down to see the city and the tower which the sons of men had built. And the LORD said, "Indeed the people are one and they all have one language, and this is what they begin to do; now nothing that they propose to do will be withheld from them. Come, let Us go down and there confuse their language, that they may not understand one another's speech." So the LORD scattered them abroad from there over the face of all the earth, and they ceased building the city. Therefore its name is called Babel, because there the LORD confused the language of all the earth; and from there the LORD scattered them abroad over the face of all the earth (11:1-9).

This is really a double etiology: it explains why Babel is named *Babel*, and why humans speak different languages. *Babel* is said to mean "confusion" in Hebrew (although the Babylonians who would one day build their capital there defined it as "gate of god"); the etiology is saying that Babel has that name because that is the place where God made it impossible for all of humanity to understand one another.

Why would God confuse everyone and give them different languages? Because, once again, humanity was trying to make themselves into gods. By trying to build "a tower whose top is in the heavens," the humans were trying to physically reach heaven and reach God. They wanted to "make a name for" themselves so they could control their own destinies instead of leaving their fates to God. Since no one person could reach heaven by him- or herself, God made it impossible for them to communicate with each other. If they couldn't talk, then they couldn't plan. If they couldn't plan, then they couldn't succeed.

Therefore, the desire to be our own gods banished us from

paradise, made our lives physically painful, and then kept us from understanding one another.

Ken Burns Cannot Supplant Your Textbooks

There is an old saying that only winners write the history books while losers write religion. It's been attributed to everyone and no one, and quite frankly, it is wrong. History books are written by writers, and Scripture was inspired by God. Only one of those two is unbiased, and it's God. History books should be about facts and not opinions, but no matter how excellent the writer, bias always creeps in somehow.

Probably the most famous historian of our time is Ken Burns. He has the distinction of directing the documentary series that knocked Carl Sagan's *Cosmos* down a peg. In 1990, *The Civil War* premiered on PBS and remains the most-watched documentary in the world; Carl Sagan's *Cosmos* is now number two.[10]

Why is Ken Burns's work so enjoyed? Because he takes history and presents it as a story with a beginning, climax, and denouement. His *Civil War* series had an inspiring theme: Americans' fight for unity. It is a theme that seamlessly translates to today, and one he knew we all needed to be reminded of. But in the quest to direct a quality documentary, some of the less exciting and more depressing details were ignored or cast in a sunnier light. For example, the Confederacy is described romantically, emphasizing the splendor of the Old South instead of the horrors of slavery, and the violence of Reconstruction following the emancipation of those slaves is barely mentioned because it betrays the series' vision of a united America after the war.[11] So was his purpose to teach the hard truths of the Civil War, or did he use the Civil War to relay a message to America? It was the latter. And there is nothing wrong with that, as long as we realize his good intentions are coloring the raw facts of history.

Just as we shouldn't replace our high school history books with a Ken Burns documentary, we don't need to look solely to the Bible for historical facts. Why not? Because God and the Bible writers had a purpose that was bigger than recording rote facts. They all had a theme to convey: God is eternally God. Writers would use the history of the Israelites to relay that message the way Burns used the history of the Civil War to encourage a unified America. Is there history in the Bible and *The Civil War*? Yes. But *are* they history? No. That's why we must have teams of less-inspired, purely fact-driven scholars writing textbooks.

So how does the Bible treat history? Is it all fiction, as many scientists would argue? Is it the only literal history, as Nathan's childhood church taught? As with most controversies, the truth lies somewhere in the middle.

Evidence of the Flood

When an archaeologist is digging in the field, nothing makes her happier than finding evidence of a fire or a flood. I know that sounds morbid, but unfortunately disasters are a great way to decide when to date artifacts. They leave identifiable layers in the soil, called *strata*, kind of like the line of buttercream in the middle of a two-layer chocolate cake. But unlike a layer cake on my countertop, soil lines can survive forever.

Arguably the greatest disaster of all time was the Flood. Floods on the scale described in Genesis 6–9 leave thick layers of mud and shell that are easy to identify. At this moment, teams of archaeologists and geologists are working all over the Near East to find unshakable evidence of Noah's Flood. Every few years there seems to be a breakthrough, only to be quietly discounted a year or so later.[12] The back-and-forth is largely a product of the number of floods that region has experienced in the last six thousand years. There are just so many flood layers to choose from.

The best extrabiblical evidence we have found for Noah's Flood isn't in the ground; it is in the literature of surrounding civilizations. If you ask me, there is no doubt the Flood happened because there are too many versions of the story that largely agree with Genesis. The most famous is the Babylonians' *Epic of Gilgamesh*. The names change, but the story is largely the same: a man and his family follow a god's instructions to save themselves (and subsequently humanity) from a flood. The Gilgamesh epic is itself a version of an earlier Akkadian story about a man whom the god instructs to build a round boat. The Sumerians and Assyrians didn't leave a flood story (at least, not that we've found yet), but they do divide their list of kings into "pre-flood" and "post-flood."[13] No doubt: there was a flood.

So who got the story right? Let's compare Genesis and Gilgamesh:

> So it came to pass, at the end of forty days, that Noah opened the window of the ark which he had made. Then he sent out a raven, which kept going to and fro until the waters had dried up from the earth. He also sent out from himself a dove, to see if the waters had receded from the face of the ground. But the dove found no resting place for the sole of her foot, and she returned into the ark to him, for the waters were on the face of the whole earth. So he put out his hand and took her, and drew her into the ark to himself. And he waited yet another seven days, and again he sent the dove out from the ark. Then the dove came to him in the evening, and behold, a freshly plucked olive leaf was in her mouth; and Noah knew that the waters had receded from the earth. So he waited yet another seven days and sent out

the dove, which did not return again to him anymore
(Genesis 8:6-12).

Six days and seven nights
came the wind and flood, the storm flattening the land...
I opened a vent and fresh air (daylight!) fell upon the
       side of my nose.
I fell to my knees and sat weeping,
tears streaming down the side of my nose.
I looked around for coastlines in the expanse of the sea,
and at twelve leagues there emerged a region (of land).
On Mt. Nimush the boat lodged firm,
Mt. Nimush held the boat, allowing no sway.
One day and a second Mt. Nimush held the boat,
       allowing no sway.
A third day, a fourth, Mt. Nimush held the boat, allowing
       no sway.
A fifth day, a sixth, Mt. Nimush held the boat, allowing
       no sway.
When a seventh day arrived
I sent forth a dove and released it.
The dove went off, but came back to me;
no perch was visible so it circled back to me.
I sent forth a swallow and released it.
The swallow went off, but came back to me;
no perch was visible so it circled back to me.
I sent forth a raven and released it.
The raven went off, and saw the waters slither back.
It eats, it scratches, it bobs, but does not circle back
       to me.[14]

These passages are the most closely related of the two texts, although the overall stories are similar. Both heroes build boats with windows and use birds to "test the waters," so to speak. Both know the flood is over when the last bird never returns. Major differences include the length of the floods (forty days vs. one week), the time of the boat's landing, and the species of the test birds.

Differences in the stories come down to, not historical accuracy, but literary purpose. The flood story in the *Epic of Gilgamesh* is a small part of the larger tale of how one man searches for immortality. The flood story in the Bible is a very, very small part of the larger tale of how humanity can be reconciled to God. The historical details, such as whether Noah loaded two of each animal (Genesis 7:8-9) or seven of some and two of others (Genesis 7:2-3), are not as important as that overall theme of reconciliation. Genesis mentions this historic event as evidence of humanity's depravity and God's enduring mercy, not to give archaeologists something else to look for in the dirt.

Reality of the Exodus

I wrote my undergraduate thesis with the intention of placing Joseph and Moses in the Egyptian calendar. I knew when I started that it was a basically impossible task, so no one was surprised when I didn't have a certain date for when the Israelites lived in Egypt. At my defense one of my advisors asked me, "So do you still believe Joseph and Moses were real?" He expected me to throw the men and my faith under the bus of secular theology.

I did not concede, and I left my advisor speechless: "I don't know exactly when the Hebrews lived in Egypt because the history and archaeology aren't definitive. But I still believe they were there because there's enough history and archaeology to hint at the Bible's truth. We haven't found it all or put it all together yet, but if we are supposed to, then we will."

To my knowledge, Ken Burns has not done a documentary about the Exodus. That's okay, because we all treat Cecil B. DeMille's *The Ten Commandments* as if it were just that: a documentary. That film has so pervaded our lives that when we read the Exodus account, we picture Moses as Charlton Heston, the unnamed pharaoh as Yul Brynner's Rameses II, and the Red Sea splitting open instantly. We picture characters who aren't in the text, such as Queen Nefertiti, and imagine episodes between her and Moses that didn't happen.

If you tried to remake *The Ten Commandments,* correcting all the historical inaccuracies, I bet you'd be branded a heretic. The first character to go would be Rameses II. The name *Rameses* is in the Bible four times (Genesis 47:11; Exodus 12:37; Numbers 33:3,5), and in each instance the name refers to a place and not a person. In fact, it is highly unlikely that Rameses II was the pharaoh of Exodus. More likely candidates lived centuries before he did, based on descriptions in the impressively detailed and rather well-preserved Egyptian records. At different times in history, the records have stories of foreign rulers taking over (à la Joseph) and slaves escaping.[15]

Few historians, and certainly no history textbook, would leave out the identity of the man who ordered all firstborn Hebrew sons to be killed. So why would Moses' own story skip it? Surely he knew who the pharaoh was, so was the name lost over centuries of oral retellings? If there is a good reason the scribes didn't record it for posterity, it must be that their goal wasn't to relay history. Could this be the ancient equivalent of newscasters refusing to name terrorists and school shooters so that the true message of Exodus—God's multiplication and salvation of His people—isn't overshadowed by the villain?

Consider this: none of the Egyptians are given names, but all of the Hebrews are—all the way down to the midwives. Most importantly, God tells His own name to Moses:

And God said to Moses, "I AM WHO I AM." And He said, "Thus you shall say to the children of Israel, 'I AM has sent me to you.'" Moreover God said to Moses, "Thus you shall say to the children of Israel: 'The LORD God of your fathers, the God of Abraham, the God of Isaac, and the God of Jacob, has sent me to you. This is My name forever, and this is My memorial to all generations'" (Exodus 3:14-15).

In the ancient world, names had power. They indicated ownership and family affiliation, but some, such as God's, were thought to have mystical powers. By knowing God's name, Moses could call on Him.

GOD'S NAME

Have you ever noticed that sometimes the name LORD is written in small caps in your Bible? Anytime you see that, the word is standing in for God's actual name, YHWH, which appears in the Hebrew text and translates to "I AM." To this day, when Jews read Scripture and see YHWH on the page, they will speak the Hebrew word that means "Lord" (*Adonai*) or "the Name" (*ha-shem*) instead of pronouncing the Divine Name. Their tradition has been adopted into our Christian Bibles; that is why we see LORD instead of *Yahweh*. Why all the hedges around God's name? Because the scribes did not want anyone reading the Bible to accidentally break the third commandment: "You shall not take the name of the LORD your God in vain" (Exodus 20:7). On the other end of the Bible, names are key to one's eternity: "He who overcomes shall be clothed in white garments, and I will not blot out his name from the Book of Life; but I will confess his name before My Father and before His angels" (Revelation 3:5).

Exodus is the story of how God fulfilled His promise to multiply the Israelites and make them His people, not the literal history of their political status and migratory patterns. By leaving the exact details of the Egypt situation fuzzy, the scribes made it easier for readers to picture themselves in the most important story of the Jewish tradition—so important that when another king was feeling threatened by a newborn who would be "King of the Jews" and ordered all male children killed, no one hesitated to compare Jesus to Moses and Herod to pharaoh (Matthew 2:16-18).

History of Politics

I am one of those people who insists on reading the book before I see a film version of the same story. This sometimes means I "discover" an author just because I think a movie looks like it will be good. Philippa Gregory was one such discovery. I knew from the previews that *The Other Boleyn Girl* was going to be a film I would love. It had it all: gorgeous clothes, handsome actors, English scenery, and the opportunity to learn some lesser-known British history.

I have since read every single one of Philippa Gregory's books in her Plantagenet and Tudor series. I have enjoyed most of them, and I've learned some history along the way. But they are not biographies, and they were not written to teach unbiased facts about the kings and queens of England. They were written to entertain people like me who enjoy a little history on the side of their romance novels. (I think it makes me feel less guilty about wasting time!)

Just because a book contains historical truth doesn't mean it is a history book. The Bible has many great examples of this. The books of Samuel and Kings are pretty much your average ancient collection of biographies. They describe events that happened in Israel while it was ruled by kings, and they tend to include it all—the good, bad, and ugly—without moralizing or judging. Chronicles, however, is not what I would call a history textbook. Yes, it contains many of the same stories we read in Samuel and Kings, but the writer of those books had a different purpose in mind when he put pen to parchment.

The Chronicler (as the writer of 1 and 2 Chronicles, Ezra, and Nehemiah is called in scholarly circles) obviously knew Israel's history, but he put his own spin on it. For example, he only included the good stories of David and Solomon. There's no murder of Bathsheba's husband (2 Samuel 11), no rape of Tamar (2 Samuel 13), and no foreign wives of Solomon (1 Kings 11:1-8).

The Chronicler was working after Jerusalem fell to the Babylonians. Likely one of the Jews returning to the city as Ezra and Nehemiah were rebuilding it, the Chronicler wanted the remaining Israelites to look back on the reigns of David and Solomon as a golden era. The times in which those two kings had lived were what the Chronicler and the rebuilders of Jerusalem were hoping to imitate with their new generation, and they knew the best way to do that was to remain in right worship of God. So the Chronicler tends to tell his stories in black and white. The "good" kings are perfect and enjoy long reigns. The "bad" kings are horrific, and they don't typically live for very long. The point the Chronicler is making is a true one that is found elsewhere in the Bible: obeying God leads to life. Of course I mean that figuratively and not (necessarily) literally, for as Paul wrote,

> And you He made alive, who were dead in trespasses and
> sins, in which you once walked according to the course
> of this world, according to the prince of the power of

the air, the spirit who now works in the sons of disobe-
dience, among whom also we all once conducted ourselves in the lusts of our flesh, fulfilling the desires of the
flesh and of the mind, and were by nature children of
wrath, just as the others.

But God, who is rich in mercy, because of His great love
with which He loved us, even when we were dead in tres-
passes, made us alive together with Christ (by grace you
have been saved), and raised us up together, and made
us sit together in the heavenly places in Christ Jesus, that
in the ages to come He might show the exceeding riches
of His grace in His kindness toward us in Christ Jesus.
For by grace you have been saved through faith, and
that not of yourselves; it is the gift of God, not of works,
lest anyone should boast. For we are His workmanship,
created in Christ Jesus for good works, which God prepared beforehand that we should walk in them (Ephesians 2:1-10).

We are all wicked human beings, but God has provided the grace
that leads to eternal life. That is the true message of the Bible.

~≋≋~

The Bible is a portrait of God, not a tool to calculate the age of
the earth or number the generations of humanity. If we expect the
Bible to be a textbook, we will be disappointed. Searching the Scriptures for validation of humanity's theories is the opposite of searching the Bible for God's face.

We have to become okay with saying, "I don't know why," when
Scripture conflicts with science and history. God does not intend
for us to know everything about Him and His creation while we are
on earth. If He did, then we would have access to that Tree of the

Knowledge of Good and Evil (Genesis 2:17)! Complete knowledge is reserved for God, and those of us who claim to have it—even on a scriptural basis—are falling into the same trap as Eve and Adam did. We find ourselves simultaneously swamped by pride in our intellects and fear of what we still don't understand.

Questions for Discussion and Reflection

1. Nowhere in God's Word can you read, "The earth is [however-many] years old as of this writing," or, "Moses and the Hebrews left Egypt on [such-and-such date]," because the Bible does not make statements of scientific or historical fact for the sake of sating human curiosity. When the world's answers don't seem to agree with the Bible's statements, can contradictory answers to life's big questions coexist as truth?

2. Why do you think God reserves a complete textbook of knowledge of science and history for Himself? If the Bible were a "teacher's manual," how would the black-and-white answers to all your questions change your faith?

Chapter 3

GEORGE WASHINGTON
WAS NO CHERRY PICKER

Washington, DC, is never more beautiful than during the annual National Cherry Blossom Festival. In 1912, Mayor Yukio Ozaki of Tokyo gave three thousand ornamental (nonfruiting) cherry trees to Washington to signify enduring friendship between our nations, and the nations have swapped cuttings back and forth ever since to keep the original trees' lineages alive in both nations.[1] The one-hundred-year-long relationship contrasts the meaning of the cherry blossoms themselves, which in Japan represent the transience of life. The ornamental cherry tree has a brief but brilliant blooming season, ended as the wind whisks the petals away. Life is beautiful but fleeting.

I incorrectly thought that Japan gave Washington, DC, all those cherry trees as a nod to the fable of George Washington cutting down his father's favorite cherry tree when he was six years old:

> When George...was about six years old, he was made
> the wealthy master of a *hatchet!* of which, like most lit-
> tle boys, he was immoderately fond, and was constantly
> going about chopping every thing that came in his

way. One day, in the garden, where he often amused himself hacking his mother's pea-sticks, he unluckily tried the edge of his hatchet on the body of a beautiful young English cherry-tree, which he barked so terribly, that I don't believe the tree ever got the better of it. The next morning the old gentleman finding out what had befallen his tree, which, by the by, was a great favourite, came into the house, and with much warmth asked for the mischievous author, declaring at the same time, that he would not have taken five guineas for his tree. Nobody could tell him any thing about it. Presently George and his hatchet made their appearance. *George,* said his father, *do you know who killed that beautiful little cherry-tree yonder in the garden?* This was a *tough question*; and George staggered under it for a moment; but quickly recovered himself: and looking at his father, with the sweet face of youth brightened with the inexpressible charm of all-conquering truth, he bravely cried out, *"I can't tell a lie, Pa; you know I can't tell a lie. I did cut it with my hatchet."–Run to my arms, you dearest boy,* cried his father in transports, *run to my arms; glad am I, George, that you killed my tree; for you have paid me for it a thousand fold. Such an act of heroism in my son, is more worth than a thousand trees, though blossomed with silver, and their fruits of purest gold.*[2]

Everyone knows this is just an anecdote meant to impress upon us the importance of truth. George Washington, father of our nation, was always honest with his own father, even when he thought he would be punished for killing what would have been a fruited cherry tree. I can only speculate as to what made it his father's favorite; maybe it provided the biggest and tastiest cherries, or maybe it was a lovely shade tree in his garden. If it had been a black cherry tree, a variety that grows wild in Virginia, at least Mr. Washington could have made some nice heirloom-quality furniture from its wood after the fictional tragedy.

There's a lot to love about the cherry tree: beautiful, nourishing, strong, metaphorical, even truthful. Not unlike our Bible.

Don't Pick, Prune, or Chop Down the Bible

As we have learned, the Bible is an anthology composed of many ancient texts written by dozens of authors over hundreds of years. All biblical stories and voices come together in a singular portrait of God and His desire to reconcile humanity to Himself. When we study and teach Scripture, each story and every voice need to be considered to extract a true interpretation of God's Word.

There are two types of preaching: proof-texting and exegesis. Whenever a preacher gets on stage or behind a pulpit and says something like, "These are the five ways the Bible tells us to do X," then you know you're about to hear some proof-texting. That person looked at the world and wondered what his or her listeners needed to hear to feel better about life. Then he went to the Bible and found passages or verses that agreed with whatever five points he wanted to make. To say this is lazy theology is an understatement, but it is probably the most popular form of Sunday-morning lecture. Sadly, many people prefer to hear only that the Bible agrees with the ways they are behaving or believing as opposed to hear just God's truth. They cherry-pick the parts of Scripture they like while undercutting God's Word as a whole.

The Method

One of the first lessons I was taught as a budding archaeologist was, "If you look for it, then you'll find it." This was in reference to excavations (and will be probed in chapter 4), but it is true for the Bible as well. If you want to "make" God validate you, then you can do it.

Let's pretend that I just found out I need to teach at a power-player women's conference in two days. It's a strange conference—one that peddles in Christian untruth—and they want me to explain why marriage is wrong. If, hypothetically, I were to accept the job (which I would never, ever do because this so obviously disagrees with God's first command in Genesis 1:28 that humanity be fruitful and multiply), then I would proof-text Scripture to make it happen. My preparation would look something like this:

Step 1: Find a nonbiblical story to introduce the topic and engage the listener.

Christina had spent the year since she had graduated from college planning her wedding. She had been hired as a congressional intern in Washington, DC, and she and her college sweetheart had decided a spring wedding under the Japanese cherry trees would be the perfect way to start their lives as a future Washington power-couple. Family and friends flew in from all over the nation to watch Christina in her blush-pink gown vow to love and honor her husband. Everything was picture-perfect that day.

Before the next spring, Christina was a mess. She was always entertaining her in-laws or cleaning for her in-laws or cooking for her in-laws. Laundry never seemed to be done, and she'd found herself working fewer hours just to keep up with personal responsibilities. She had been passed over for a promotion, and now her husband wanted to add a baby to the chaos. Married life was no bowl full of cherries. She'd lost her ambitions, her successfulness, and herself—all because she'd tied herself to one good-looking guy.

Step 2: Break the topic down into three-to-five points.

Christina's story exemplifies the three reasons the Bible doesn't want women to marry:

1. The domestic responsibilities associated with marriage are all-consuming.
2. Marriage distracts women from reaching their God-given potential.
3. Marriage makes women shallow and sex-addicted.

Step 3: Cherry-pick Bible verses that support the points.

Let's look at the verses that tell us why women shouldn't marry:

1. Proverbs 31:10: "Who can find a virtuous wife? / For her worth is far above rubies..." The list of wives' responsibilities is so long it must be a sarcastic way of reminding women they don't want those responsibilities.
2. Matthew 19:12 (THE VOICE): "Others have renounced marriage for the sake of the kingdom of heaven. Anyone who can embrace that call should do so." Women should model other single women who live happy, charitable lives.
3. 1 Corinthians 7:34: "The unmarried woman cares about the things of the Lord, that she may be holy both in body and in spirit. But she who is married cares about the things of the world—how she may please her husband." Wives get distracted by all the daily household and nightly sexual responsibilities. Those women can no longer love God.

This exaggerated little exercise was honestly painful to write because it is so disrespectful of Scripture. Because the verses are taken out of context—the contexts of the Bible as a whole, the books they are in, and in some cases the very sentences around them—the words can be used to justify just about any claim.

If women were to listen to a speech like the one outlined above and then decide not to marry—or worse, divorce—then they would be falling victim to false teaching and believing in false theology. Sadly, this has been happening to Christians since the very day the Christ was resurrected, as supposed believers doubted His return (1 Corinthians 15:12).

False Beliefs

The consequences of false teachings can be devastating and far-reaching, impacting not only individuals' choices but the behaviors and beliefs of entire societies. Up until the eighteenth century, proof-texting was complicit in the continuation of slavery in Europe and the New World. Proponents would point to the Bible and say, "Abraham had slaves" (Genesis 21:9-10), and "God never disapproved of it in the law" (Exodus 20:8-10,17). You would think the average Christian would hear that reasoning and respond, "But that was before Jesus came and fulfilled the law," but the New Testament didn't exactly outlaw slavery either. Jesus did not condemn the practice in the Gospels, and Paul actually told slaves to obey their masters (Ephesians 6:5-8).

If you look at only those four points, then it does seem as if the Bible makes a case in support of slavery. But consider the contexts. Scripture is written for humanity living in an imperfect fallen world. Institutions exist here that God does not support, but God's displeasure doesn't make them cease to exist. God addressed slavery in the law because it was part of the human condition, much as He gave instructions for divorce. Consider what happened in Mark 10:2-12:

> The Pharisees came and asked Him, "Is it lawful for a man to divorce his wife?" testing Him.
>
> And He answered and said to them, "What did Moses command you?"
>
> They said, "Moses permitted a man to write a certificate of divorce, and to dismiss her."
>
> And Jesus answered and said to them, "Because of the hardness of your heart he wrote you this precept. But from the beginning of the creation, God 'made them male and female.' 'For this reason a man shall leave his father and mother and be joined to his wife, and the two shall become one flesh'; so then they are no longer two, but one flesh. Therefore what God has joined together, let not man separate."
>
> In the house His disciples also asked Him again about the same matter. So He said to them, "Whoever divorces his wife and marries another commits adultery against her. And if a woman divorces her husband and marries another, she commits adultery."

God gave all of those 613 laws to Moses and the wandering Israelites because humans needed them to navigate the flawed world God never intended for us. At first, He had one rule: don't eat from the tree of knowledge. After we broke that rule, He made adjustments and added rules to keep humanity going until Jesus could bring God's people back into a right, pre-Fall relationship with Him.

As Paul was writing just after Jesus' resurrection, slavery was still common all over the world. (It takes generations for human institutions to change; slavery would be legal in Europe and America for another eighteen hundred years.) Although Jesus' gospel message disagreed with slavery, His words had not yet penetrated society. After explaining to new Christians how the law worked, Paul then mentioned that flawed institution of slavery in Galatians 3:26-28 simply because it still existed: "You are all sons of God through faith in Christ Jesus. For as many of you as were baptized into Christ have put on Christ. There is neither Jew nor Greek, there is neither slave nor free, there is neither male nor female; for you are all one in Christ Jesus." Just because slavery once existed, that doesn't make it right. There should be no categories of "slave" and "free" because all who accept Jesus' sacrifice are children—princes and princesses—of God.

But just because God's children are all princes and princesses in His kingdom, that doesn't mean we are all wealthy and healthy here on earth. Contrary to the claims of too many rich and famous pastors with gigantic followings, a right relationship with God does *not* guarantee earthly comforts. The only way you end up believing that is with proof-texting.

There are two common themes among the various prosperity theologians: (1) if you are suffering, then you don't have enough faith; (2) if you are poor, then you don't have enough faith. Before we get into the actual false theology of these claims, just read them again. Those statements are about you, you, you, and you. No God. No Jesus.

No one wants to suffer. But since we humans decided to have our eyes opened so we could "be like God, knowing good *and evil*" (Genesis 3:5, emphasis added), we've been stuck with both. There was a reason God didn't want us eating from that tree: He didn't intend for us to suffer evil. And Scripture actually tells us—rather consistently throughout the New Testament—that those who are closest to God suffer the most. In other words, the more faith you have, the more likely you are to suffer. But I guess that isn't the kind of message that packs amphitheaters with tithing listeners.

Consider what happened to all the men who were the very closest to Jesus, the apostles. With the exception of John, who died while exiled for his faith in Jesus, every single one of them was executed because of his great faith. Those stories come to us from Christian tradition and history, but Scripture agrees that those with the greatest faith have the hardest lives, and it actually foreshadows their fates. Faith didn't save Paul from suffering; it helped him through it. The knowledge of the faith *of others*, in fact, helped him survive:

> We told you before when we were with you that we would suffer tribulation, just as it happened, and you know. For this reason, when I could no longer endure [suffering], I sent to know [the state of your faith]...But now that Timothy has come to us from you, and brought us good news of your faith and love, and that you always have good remembrance of us, greatly desiring to see us, as we also to see you—therefore, brethren, in all our affliction and distress we were comforted concerning you by your faith. For now we live, if you stand fast in the Lord (1 Thessalonians 3:4-8).

One sort of suffering, which prosperity theologians tend to elevate to the number-one indicator of the health of your relationship with God, is financial poverty. If you are poor, then it is because you don't have enough faith that God will bless you with more money. (The cynic in me would add, "with more money...that you can give to those false theologians' churches.") The absolute absurdity of the claim that faith yields wealth cannot be overstated.

Let's go straight to Jesus' mouth to find out how God feels about the impoverished. In the Gospel of Luke, the first time Jesus speaks in public, He reads from the book of Isaiah:

> "The Spirit of the LORD is upon Me,
> Because He has anointed Me
> To preach the gospel to the poor;
> He has sent Me to heal the brokenhearted,
> To proclaim liberty to the captives
> And recovery of sight to the blind,
> To set at liberty those who are oppressed;
> To proclaim the acceptable year of the LORD."
> Then He closed the book, and gave it back to the
>   attendant and sat down (Luke 4:18-20).

The very first people Jesus mentions are the poor. And He is there to tell them His good news, not to make them wealthy. Whenever Jesus mentions the poor, His concern is for their spiritual wealth, not their monetary wealth. He never shames them for lack of faith or blames them for their financial status. In fact, He reminds them of a bright side: they are more likely to have the greatest faith! Jesus tells His disciples, "Blessed are you poor, for yours is the kingdom of God" (Luke 6:20); the kingdom belongs to the poor and not the wealthy.

Paul reinforces this time and again. Although he sometimes uses physical wealth as a metaphor (making his words susceptible to out-of-context proof-texting), it is obvious that it is meant to represent spiritual well-being because Jesus Himself was never literally wealthy. Paul writes, "I speak not by commandment, but I am testing the sincerity of your love by the diligence of others. For you know the grace of our Lord Jesus Christ, that though He was rich, yet for your sakes He became poor, that you through His poverty might become rich" (2 Corinthians 8:8-9).

So if faith doesn't make you wealthy and healthy here on earth, as some proof-texters would have you believe, then what does it do?

> Therefore, *having been justified by faith, we have peace* with God through our Lord Jesus Christ, through whom also we have *access by faith into this grace* in which we stand, and rejoice *in hope of the glory of God*. And not only that, but we also *glory in tribulations*, knowing that *tribulation produces perseverance; and perseverance, character; and character, hope.* Now hope does not disappoint, because the love of God has been poured out in our hearts by the Holy Spirit who was given to us (Romans 5:1-5, emphasis added).

Paul's letter to the Roman Christians is unique among his writings. At the time it was sent, he had never visited the Roman church or modeled evangelism for them. He did not know its leaders the way he did in Corinth, Philippi, and the other recipient cities, so he presented the gospel message to them with the purpose of preparing them to take Jesus' good news to all of Italy and Spain.

Faith is a frequent topic in Romans, but never is it impetus for earthly reward. Faith, as Paul describes in chapter 5, results in "peace with God," "grace," and "hope of the glory of God." Faith allows us to "glory in tribulations" because they improve our "character" and give us even more "hope." There's no *health* or *wealth* mentioned there—quite the opposite, in fact. You won't find false theologians quoting those verses if they want to increase their followings and receipts.

Climb into the Bible and Stay Awhile

Exegesis is a type of study that starts with Scripture, and then lets the Holy Spirit reveal God's truths. It doesn't require concordances or indexes, wild ideas or personal conjecture. Just prayer, time in the Bible, and a willingness to change.

A mentor of mine who attended seminary several decades ago tells the story of his first experience with exegesis. Frank had a professor who, at the start of the term, gave his students one Bible verse. They were told to go home that night and write down ten observations about the text. They weren't allowed to consult outside materials for ideas or add verses to make the passage longer. It was challenging for such a short passage, but the assignment was worse after the next class and then the next, as they repeated the exercise—without making any duplicate observations—every day for the semester. By Christmas, the students all had notebooks full of thoughts about that one verse, and all agreed that meditating on Scripture as they had done allowed it to speak in ways they never would have heard without such detailed attention.

Frank has delivered my favorite sermons of all time. For a series of Sundays, he would pick a book of the Bible and recite it from beginning to end. He did it dynamically, pausing where he needed to explain historical or textual or literary contexts that informed the meanings of the words. He doesn't speak as much as he used to, but he still makes a habit of memorizing books of the Bible, not just verses. I know John 3:16, which is fine, but he knows John. Why? Because Scripture cannot be properly understood in a vacuum. What John wrote from 1:1 to 3:15 and 3:17 to 21:25 colors his words in verse 16.

These are the two parts of exegesis: attention to detail and knowledge of context.

The Method

Whenever David and I have hosted small-group Bible studies, our most successful ones (based on attendance, enthusiasm, and overall *aha* moments) were when the group decided on a book of the Bible and just started reading. At each meeting I tended to facilitate the discussions, filling in mainly historical context where necessary and answering the occasional question if I could. We left each meeting with a loose assignment to read the next chapter or so of text and write down observations and questions to discuss the next time.

We tended to select narrative books for study, such as Esther, because they were entertaining and already familiar to everyone at the table. This was good for me, too, because it was easy for me to prepare historical, textual, and literary details I could share with the group to broaden their understandings of the passages. My goal was always to help everyone see past the limitations of their English translations and understand the world from which the story was written. I wanted context to help them interpret Scripture themselves, not make them all believe as I believe and take my word as gospel.

So let's take one of those proof-texted verses from page 79 and exegete it instead. (If I haven't stepped on your toes yet in this chapter, then I'm about to.)

Proverbs 31:10-31 has become the go-to passage for many Christian married women. On the surface and out of context, it is the laundry list (pun intended) of activities, attitudes, and accolades women should be attempting. They include:

- making her husband feel secure about their relationship,
- feeding and clothing her family and employees,
- running a small vineyard and winery,
- sleeping no more than one REM cycle each night,
- volunteering to help the poor,

- keeping up on the latest fashions,
- making her husband famous, and
- sharing her wisdom and kindness with everyone.

Easy-peasy! Nothing about that list is at all intimidating or makes me feel like a failure as a woman.

I thank God He did not finish the book of Proverbs with a poem about how I should behave in my marriage, because David does all the grocery shopping, I sleep ten hours every night if I can manage it, and my daily work uniform consists of clean-but-paint-splattered T-shirts and faded yoga pants. Part of the reason David feels so secure in our relationship (he says I tick that box!) just might be my stereotypical work-at-home writer sloppiness and not the love and affection I shower upon him.

Step 1: Textual Criticism

I like to begin studying a text by figuring out who wrote the passage and when and where he did so. When it comes to Proverbs, this may be a bit harder than it initially looks. The book begins by saying, "The proverbs of Solomon the son of David, king of Israel," which readers traditionally take to mean that Solomon is the author. For a lot of reasons—foremost among them the construction of the text (which we will get to next)—that first "of" likely means something more like "inspired by" or even "commissioned by." Proverbs is probably not *by* Solomon, but because he was known as a wise king, the book was dedicated to him.

In the Hebrew, it is easier to tell that Proverbs is an anthology of several collections of sayings. Some of these collections are directly attributed to their authors (such as the "men of Hezekiah" in 25:1); others were written or collected by a more general "Teacher" of young men. Proverbs 31 says it is the collected sayings of King

Lemuel's mother to her son, as told by King Lemuel to the Teacher who compiled all the sayings.

WHAT IS THE BEST BIBLE TRANSLATION?

I first asked that question of a theology professor when I was a freshman in undergrad. The response stung: "No translation will ever be good enough." Her implied but unstated next thought was, *So go sign up for Hebrew and Greek next semester*. At that point I still thought I'd become a lawyer or architect, so it would be another year before I entered Intro to Biblical Hebrew.

The thing is, she was right. If you don't know the original languages, then you are stuck relying upon someone else's translation that may or may not be correct.

But let's be practical: most Christians aren't going to learn Hebrew or Greek because they are too busy (hopefully) showing the gospel to the world. I think God would rather have most of us "in the field" than behind desks squinting at jots and tittles. He gifted certain people for that, and many of them are the very ones doing the translations. So when people ask me, "What is the best translation?" I try not to shut them down with a holier-than-thou deflection.

You might not know the original languages, but you can know who translated your Bible and what decisions they made. Did a church or denomination sponsor the translation? Was it the work of just one person; if so, what does he or she believe? When ancient manuscripts disagreed, which one was translated in that version and why? Answering these questions isn't such a hard assignment, and their answers can make you trust the translation (or translations) you choose to read. Just look at the Bible version's introduction. All you need to know should be there.

Step 2: Historical Criticism

Although Proverbs contains wisdom from before Babylonia con-quered Jerusalem in 586 BCE, the book was more likely compiled from oral tradition and edited after the exile, at least one hundred years later. This is largely based on the setting of Proverbs, which is a school. Young men would have gathered in a small group to learn from an older man, usually a scribe.[3]

It is true: if someone was educated in Israel, he was male. The ancient world was ruled by men; if you doubt that, just read your Bible. Male-dominated societies are called *patriarchies*, and that is exactly what Israel was. God is "Father," not "Mother." The oldest son, not the oldest child, gets the largest inheritance. Ruling mon-archs were kings, not queens. You don't have to like it, but you need to accept that it is true.

Right there, at the intersection of ancient patriarchy and mod-ern feminism, is where misinterpretation of Proverbs 31 begins. When women read the Bible for role models, we instinctively look for feminine pronouns. Many books have been written about how poorly women are treated in the Scriptures. They are sometimes sacrificed and raped, often marginalized and unnamed, and in our zeal to find and get to know characters "like us" in Scripture, we sometimes invent names for them. Since the fourth century, the woman with the issue of blood (Luke 8:43-48) has been known at different times and in different places as Veronica and Bernice and even Martha of Bethany. More recently, feminist scholars have named women to make them more relatable and dignified. Cheryl Exum, for example, named the raped and dismembered Levite wife of Judges 19 Bath-sheber.[4] The desire for more female biblical role models is nothing new.

Women and men need to look beyond the gender of biblical characters because modern gender roles do not match ancient ones. (Again, I'm not saying you have to like it, but you do have to admit that it is true.) Looking at that proverbial laundry list again, my husband ticks as many of the "perfect wife" boxes as I do. He makes me feel secure about our relationship, keeps me fed and clothed, volunteers in the community, and is far more fashionable than I am on a daily basis. On the other hand, I have a higher educational degree than David does. I am more likely to be a leader, and he can't touch me when it comes to the traditionally male pastimes of grilling, gardening, and gutter-cleaning. (And he doesn't want to!)

All that to say, when just about anyone is reading the Bible today, he or she is more likely to have more in common with a male character than a female character. In the book of Proverbs, women should not identify with the popularly named Woman of Virtue in 31:10-31; we are actually the students being taught the lessons of wisdom and folly by the Teacher.

Step 3: Literary Criticism

So if women aren't supposed to emulate the Woman of Virtue as described at the end of Proverbs, then what are we supposed to get out of that final poem?

All of the proverbs were collected and taught to encourage students to seek God throughout their lives, and much of the book is concerned with the dichotomy between wisdom and folly. These traits are personified in Proverbs, rendered in The Voice translation as "Lady Wisdom" and "Lady Folly." Lady Wisdom is depicted as an unmarried woman reaching out to young suitors, and men are encouraged throughout Proverbs to follow the path of Lady

Wisdom, which leads to God. She is challenged by Lady Folly, who reaches out to the same men in insidious ways. The virtues of the former and vices of the latter are emphasized in Proverbs.

The last twenty-one verses of Proverbs—the very passage that women have used to judge themselves and one another for centuries—is actually the conclusion to the struggle between Wisdom and Folly for the hearts of humanity. Here, Wisdom, the victor, is depicted as a married woman. The students who followed her would be rewarded with happiness, which men in the ancient world apparently defined as security, success, wealth, respect...and awesome wardrobes.

Happiness is every man *and woman's* reward for pursing wisdom instead of folly.

Step 4: Read the Scripture slowly and carefully.

Once the context of a passage has been evaluated from all angles—historical, textual, and literary—it is time to zoom in, take out our notebooks, and write down hundreds of observations about each verse. See if you can beat Frank's and his classmates' records!

Just kidding. Careful inspection of God's Word is central to exegesis, but you would miss so much of the Bible if you spent six months on every verse. If you could live to one hundred and had come out of the womb fully literate, you'd still read only 200 of the 31,102 verses (give or take, depending on which Bible you are reading). That is 13 percent of Genesis and only .65 percent of God's Word. Clearly there has to be a balance between studying the minutia and the big picture of Scripture.

As an example of how to read the Bible slowly and carefully, let's settle into just one verse of the Virtuous Woman poem:

> She girds herself with strength,
> And strengthens her arms

(Proverbs 31:17).

My first question would be, who is "she"? From literary context, we know this is the personification of Lady Wisdom as a queen mother's ideal daughter-in-law.

What on earth does "girds" mean? In the Bible, you'll often see that word in combination with "his loins" and in a war setting. In English, you'll see that word as the first part of *girdle*. To *gird* is to encircle something. Warriors would wrap their abdomens (specifically the muscles on either side of the spinal column) before a battle to protect their vital organs. Women, millennia later, would wrap the same area with torture devices that used bone stays and rigid fabric to cinch their waistlines (not much organ protection happening there!). The Virtuous Woman is wrapping herself firmly and tightly. The writer probably did have the warrior's girdle in mind when he recorded this, so if you're picturing someone like the Greek goddess Athena, that's not too far off.

How can one be wrapped "with strength"? The woman isn't protecting herself with armor or any other material object. If I go to the Hebrew-English lexicon, I learn that the Hebrew word translated as "strength" here means literal physical muscle power. The following verb form does as well. This woman is physically active. Maybe she's doing the ancient Israelite equivalent of PiYo or Pure Barre to strengthen her core?

If she is strengthening "herself," then why are her arms singled out? Arms are used here to reinforce her strength and authority. Other versions of this Hebrew word refer to military forces, so again, a kind of administrative strength surrounds this physically strong character.

If we were to detail the surrounding verses, we would learn that she works with her hands a lot. The woman plants her own vineyard

(v. 16); she makes her own threads (v. 19) before sewing her own clothes and housewares (v. 22). She has servants and family members who follow her every instruction (vv. 15,27). Strength is central to her lifestyle and an integral part of her body, just as strength always complements the virtue of wisdom.

The Result

When the Bible is exegeted instead of proof-texted, God's words can have a totally different meaning. What is obvious to a casual English reader—that mothers such as King Lemuel's have impossibly high standards for their future daughters-in-law—is turned upside down when historical, textual, and literary contexts are considered in combination with careful reading.

Our hypothetical friend Christina doesn't need to stress out about her cooking and housekeeping and future childrearing; she can focus on what God has planned for her specific life that will honor Him. Maybe it's wife- and motherhood, or maybe it's a power career. Maybe both. From any and all of those positions, she can serve God with wisdom. And that godly service will bring her happiness.

The Impact

Wisdom is just as much a reward for the faithfulness and good choices of women as it is for men. One of the first lessons we can take from that truth is not to judge ourselves or other women by impossible standards. I shouldn't judge David based on whether or not he can write a book, and thankfully David doesn't judge me on whether or not I can read a blueprint. God uses everyone differently in His work to reconcile all of humanity to Himself, and He offers wisdom to all who will follow Him.

The Bible is not just a collection of cherry-sized memory verses that are ripe for picking only when they validate our own opinions; it is a strong and beautiful reflection of God, and all parts of it are part of Him. Let's not take George Washington's proverbial hatchet to Scripture by proof-texting God's words to justify human ideas rather than God's. That would leave us with dead faiths in false theologies that are contrary to God's character.

Instead, let us learn about the Scriptures—their historical, textual, and literary contexts—as we study the words themselves. This holistic approach to the Bible gives us a more complete picture of God, Jesus, and the Holy Spirit—and the world that wrote down Their words for us.

Questions for Discussion and Reflection

1. A deep study of Scripture ideally includes an investment of time in learning the historical, textual, and literary contexts of passages. Why is such exegetical study preferable to skimming only English translations or cherry-picking parts of the Bible you enjoy the most?

2. No longer do Westerners live in a patriarchal society that defines roles based on biological gender alone; in fact, more women graduate today with advanced degrees than do their male counterparts. In the twenty-first century, might you also identify with biblical characters who share your societal station and cultural responsibilities and not just your gender?

Chapter 4

INDIANA JONES AND THE BURIED SCRIPTURES

Go to Israel in the summer, and you'll meet dozens of archaeologists with "The Raiders March" as their ringtones. Yes, even I had that *Indiana Jones* theme song on my phone when I was in grad school, and I wasn't even born until a week after the movie was released in theaters. Cliché as it may be, biblical archaeologists do imagine themselves as Indiana Jones stand-ins, discovering relics so powerful that they melt the faces off Nazi soldiers.[1]

The reality of archaeological work isn't so glamorous. Everyone wakes up about 4:00 in the morning, eats cold cereal, then stumbles bleary-eyed to the site just before sunrise. Depending on the day, one might do heavy work with a pickaxe or detailed work with a brush, trying to unearth artifacts as gently but efficiently as possible. Around 9:00 everyone stops for "second breakfast" (Hobbits have nothing on archaeologists!), then work continues until the heat of the day hits just after noon. It is hot, dry, heavy, tedious work, and for every five hundred pieces of broken pottery the team uncovers, there might be one object of interest.

Of course, an archaeologist's work doesn't stop at noon. After a few hours of siesta in the afternoon, occupied by showers, lunch, and naps, everyone returns to the site to wash the day's finds, sort out the "diagnostic" pieces from the unhelpful ones, catalog them, and photograph them. Then it's back to the campsite (or dorms or hotel, if you're lucky) for dinner, a call home, and a well-deserved night's sleep. This is life for six days a week, two-to-three months out of the year.

While the search for the ark of the covenant continues here in the real world, everyday discoveries help readers to understand the cultures that produced the Bible's otherwise-untranslatable or unimaginable imagery. Ever wondered what the golden calf looked like (Exodus 32)? A similar one was found in Ashkelon.[2] What about those "five-sided doorposts" (1 Kings 6:31 THE VOICE) leading to the holy of holies in Solomon's temple? A shrine at Qeiyafa has the answer.[3] No evil armies were burned alive in the discovery of those artifacts, but they do make understanding Scripture easier and more fun.

Let's peek at what life looked like in ancient Israel. Temples, cities, houses—even gates—bore no resemblance to the churches, neighborhoods, homes, and security systems we enjoy in the twenty-first century. I think you'll be surprised at just how much a knowledge of ancient art and architecture can change what we think we know about the Bible.

Religious Life

One of the richest areas for biblical archaeology outside of Israel is Syria. Correction: *was* Syria. During the civil war that continues, as of this writing, to ravage the country, ISIS has destroyed some or all parts of the nation's six World Heritage sites, including Aleppo (an ancient Hittite, then Aramean city) and Damascus (the ancient capital of Aram). Both cities were conquered by the Assyrian Empire around the same time that Northern Israel fell to them in 722 BCE. ISIS has looted the areas, sold artifacts on the black market, and then destroyed ancient temples, cities, and archaeological parks in the name of their religion.

I was heartbroken when I learned that the temple at Ain Dara in Syria had been attacked. Between January 20 and January 22, 2018, the Turkish air force deliberately struck the site twice using GPS-guided precision munitions, destroying the iconic giant footprints that had been carved into the temple stairs around 1000 BCE. It cannot be determined if the site itself was targeted for cultural or religious reasons, or if an ISIS militant cell organized there in hopes that the site's historical significance would keep them from being targeted.[4] Either way, the world has lost a treasure.

The temple at Ain Dara was the closest thing we had on earth to Solomon's temple. It was built and used around the same time, it matched the Bible's descriptions of the Israelite temple's layout, and it was decorated with carvings of cherubim. Don't think this means King Solomon stole the blueprints for his temple from the Hittites who had built Ain Dara. Instead, the similarities indicate a common architectural aesthetic throughout the ancient Near East.

Think of it as you would original craftsman-style houses: they are all over the United States and were built within decades of each other, but each was tailored to fit its owners' needs. It may have been popular in 1000 BCE for temples to have three chambers, carvings of monsters, and an elevated holy of holies, but Ain Dara (and other similar temples in the region) was specifically fashioned for a Hittite god while Solomon's temple was for Yahweh.

Temple Art

If the word *cherub* has you picturing Anne Geddes's portraits of babies on clouds or the Sistine Chapel's paintings of toddlers with wings, then I need to burst your bubble. Cherubim (that's the plural of *cherub*) aren't watchful guardian angels who bring peace and joy, love and happiness. They are monsters. Fully formed, totally terrifying monsters. The chubby babies are actually called *putti* and became popular during the Renaissance. They have no place in Scripture whatsoever.

Solomon's temple was decorated with carvings of cherubim, and according to the prophet's vision of God's throne room in Isaiah 6, seraphim were there too. Cherubim are present all over the ancient Near East. They are amalgamations of animals, usually with lion bodies, eagle wings, and human heads. The biblical versions also have calves' hooves (Ezekiel 1:7).

The cherubim, or "living creatures" as they are described in Ezekiel and Revelation, are like God's mascots. They appear wherever He is, and most importantly, they form His throne. They sit atop the ark of the covenant, which God uses as His footstool. In the ancient Near East, gods were often associated with certain animals. For example, Baal was usually depicted in paintings, reliefs, or sculptures seated on a bull calf. This fact might shed new light on the classic "golden calf" story of Exodus 32.

> Now when the people saw that Moses delayed coming down from the mountain, the people gathered together to Aaron, and said to him, "Come, make us gods that shall go before us; for as for this Moses, the man who brought us up out of the land of Egypt, we do not know what has become of him."
>
> And Aaron said to them, "Break off the golden earrings which are in the ears of your wives, your sons, and your daughters, and bring them to me." So all the people

broke off the golden earrings which were in their ears, and brought them to Aaron. And he received the gold from their hand, and he fashioned it with an engraving tool, and made a molded calf.

Then they said, "This is your god, O Israel, that brought you out of the land of Egypt!"

So when Aaron saw it, he built an altar before it. And Aaron made a proclamation and said, "Tomorrow is a feast to the LORD." Then they rose early on the next day, offered burnt offerings, and brought peace offerings; and the people sat down to eat and drink, and rose up to play (Exodus 32:1-6).

Consider for a moment that Cecil B. DeMille's imagining of the Israelites in *The Ten Commandments* melting down their gold earrings and casting a golden calf wasn't actually the wild pagan party he put on film. (For one thing, just a bunch of earrings would never make something the size DeMille imagined.) Maybe they weren't trying to make a god for themselves but were trying to bring Yahweh back to them.

The Israelites were scared. At the time of the casting, Moses had been up on the mountain so long that everyone thought he was dead (Exodus 32:1). Obviously they'd lost faith in God's and Moses' promises to them, so they tried to take matters into their own hands. By leaning on the worship practices of other civilizations—such as the Egyptians' whom they had just left—it is possible Aaron intended to cast a throne for their unseen God. He did not mold God, as Canaanite worshippers would mold Baal atop his bull, but only His mount. Could Aaron have been trying to call God down to them (v. 4)? Could the Israelites have been worshipping their "unseen God" above the small calf they'd made (v. 6)? The text seems to support this interpretation because the feast day they were honoring was Yahweh's, not a calf's. We would *never* make a molten image of God—that's just stupid, right?—but would we try to entice Him down to us when we feel abandoned? Absolutely.

We can see what that calf might have looked like thanks to an archaeological discovery at Ashkelon, Israel. A silver-plated bronze calf (4.5 inches long, 4.5 inches tall, and weighing under one pound) dated to the 1500s BCE was uncovered with its clay shrine in that port city. It likely predated the arrival of the conquering Philistines (whose provenance remains mysterious) by at least three hundred years, and thus could have been in use by the resident Canaanites as the Israelites were wandering the area with Moses.

Notice how quickly God followed the golden-calf debacle with the making of His ark of the covenant. He renews His covenant with the wishy-washy often-faithless Israelites, then sets about giving them something physical to represent His presence. God instructs the Israelites to build a tent for Him where He can meet with Moses closer to the camps, and then to craft the ark and its golden double-cherubim-topped cover (Exodus 34–37). Wherever the ark would rest—in that tent or later in the temple—God would "sit" above the cherubim's wings. And the people had a place to look for Him.

About a millennium later, when the Northern Kingdom of Israel was about to be conquered by the Assyrians, the prophet Isaiah had a vision of God enthroned above cherubim in a temple. But some other monsters were there too: seraphim. And like the cherubim, these were not humans with wings.

Archaeologists have found images of winged snakes throughout the ancient Near East, most pertinently on a seal that belonged to an Israelite temple priest.[5] Monsters such as the cherub and the seraph were considered divine guardians in the ancient world; that is why they are found in temples—to warn people away from power of the supernatural. As winged poisonous serpents, the creature who is cursed by God to move "on your belly" and "eat dust all the days of your life" after tempting Eve (Genesis 3:14) just might have been a seraph. Having disobeyed God, he was "cut down to the ground," as Lucifer had been cast out of heaven (Isaiah 14:12). We are never told why the serpent appeared where he did in the garden, so it is worth considering that he may have been stationed at the tree of knowledge to keep the humans away from it, as God would later station cherubim east of Eden after he expelled Adam and Eve (Genesis 3:24).

Temple Furnishings

The ark of the covenant, though the most important part of Solomon's temple, was not the only thing inside. When the temple was active, it was a place of constant offering to God. The gifts may have been unleavened bread, wine, incense, or animal sacrifices. The priests who ran the temple needed all sorts of furniture and tools to keep the temple running, including various types of carts, basins, stands, and altars. Since none of us regularly give offerings of anything other than money and time, the technical descriptions of those pieces in Scripture do not naturally draw mental pictures for us.

Consider this description of a cart that would have been used to roll sacrifices around Solomon's temple:

> This was the design of the carts: They had panels, and the panels were between frames; on the panels that were between the frames were lions, oxen, and cherubim. And on the frames was a pedestal on top. Below the lions and oxen were wreaths of plaited work. Every cart had four bronze wheels and axles of bronze, and its four feet had supports. Under the laver were supports

of cast bronze beside each wreath. Its opening inside
the crown at the top was one cubit in diameter; and the
opening was round, shaped like a pedestal, one and a
half cubits in outside diameter; and also on the opening
were engravings, but the panels were square, not round
(1 Kings 7:28-31).

Thanks to archaeology, we know what those looked like because
similar items have been found during the excavations of surrounding cultures. In 1990, Trude Dothan excavated cart parts that nearly
match that description at the Philistine city of Ekron, which was
only about twenty-five miles from its contemporary city of Jerusalem. The Philistine carts would have been in use within one hundred years of Solomon's temple carts, so like the bronze calf found
at another Philistine city, they are likely similar to what the Bible
describes.[6] Similar items have been found all over the ancient Near
East, especially in Cyprus.

Another common furnishing that would have been used in Solomon's temple was the altar for sacrifices. We find two different
descriptions of it in Exodus:

An altar of earth you shall make for Me, and you shall
sacrifice on it your burnt offerings and your peace offerings, your sheep and your oxen. In every place where
I record My name I will come to you, and I will bless
you. And if you make Me an altar of stone, you shall
not build it of hewn stone; for if you use your tool on
it, you have profaned it. Nor shall you go up by steps to
My altar, that your nakedness may not be exposed on it
(Exodus 20:24-26).

You shall make an altar of acacia wood, five cubits long
and five cubits wide—the altar shall be square—and

its height shall be three cubits. You shall make its horns on its four corners; its horns shall be of one piece with it. And you shall overlay it with bronze. Also you shall make its pans to receive its ashes, and its shovels and its basins and its forks and its firepans; you shall make all its utensils of bronze. You shall make a grate for it, a network of bronze; and on the network you shall make four bronze rings at its four corners. You shall put it under the rim of the altar beneath, that the network may be midway up the altar. And you shall make poles for the altar, poles of acacia wood, and overlay them with bronze. The poles shall be put in the rings, and the poles shall be on the two sides of the altar to bear it. You shall make it hollow with boards; as it was shown you on the mountain, so shall they make it (Exodus 27:1-8).

The first altar description was given before the Israelites had been told to build a traveling tent for God. Since they did not yet have permanent items they carried with them everywhere, it makes sense that a simple earthen altar could have been easily built and left behind wherever they camped. The second altar is described as much more ornate and fully portable. It would have been a better fit with all of the tent's bronze (and later temple's gold) metal-plated furnishings and tools.

Altars were used only by the priests. There they would perform animal sacrifices, pour out liquid offerings, and burn grain offerings. The horns, one on each corner, were the most sacred part of the altars, although their function is still unknown. I imagine they would tie large sacrifices to the horns, as is mentioned in Psalm 118:27, but it is possible the horns were simply symbolic. Whenever someone "took hold of the horns of the altar" as Adonijah did in 1 Kings 1:50, he was to be granted asylum regardless of the crime committed:

> Now Adonijah was afraid of Solomon; so he arose, and went and took hold of the horns of the altar. And it was told Solomon, saying, "Indeed Adonijah is afraid of King Solomon; for look, he has taken hold of the horns of the altar, saying, 'Let King Solomon swear to me today that he will not put his servant to death with the sword'" (1 Kings 1:50-51).

In this case grasping the horns did not work. Solomon had Adonijah, his older brother and rival for David's throne, executed.

It is amazing that any earthen or even thinly plated wooden altars would survive thousands of years, but one hornless earthen altar remains at Arad. Most of the other altars that have been found in Israel are stone—hewn stone that God prohibited in Exodus 20:25. The most famous example of a four-horned altar was found at Beer-Sheva. Three loose horns, which theoretically had been dismantled during Hezekiah's reforms in the late 700s BCE, were excavated there and are now on display at the Israel Museum. As a way of bringing Judah back into right worship of God, King Hezekiah ordered all worship sites other than Solomon's temple be destroyed (2 Kings 18:4).[7] In Beer-Sheva, at least, it seems his orders were followed.

City Life

The temple may be the most famous of Solomon's building projects, but some of his other lesser-known city structures can still be toured in Israel. Remains of his walls and gates and storehouses are studded all over Israel, and his greatest cities of Hazor, Megiddo, and Gezer still have signs of the chariot fleets and stabled horses he deployed from them.

National Defense

The first responsibility of any ruler is the security of his people, and Solomon was one great defender. He was certainly not the first judge or king of Israel to fortify and develop his cities, but he seems to have been the most prolific.

The walls that surrounded Solomon's cities were not just one or two layers of concrete block as you might imagine. Casemate walls were cheaper, stronger, and more useful than that; they stood in Judah until Jerusalem was razed by the Babylonians in 586 BCE. A *casemate* was formed when two parallel walls that doubly enclose a city were connected by perpendicular sections of wall every so often. The cells (casemates) made within the two parallel walls were sometimes filled in with rubble for extra protection, or they could be used for storage.

In the story of the Israelites' conquest of Jericho in Joshua 2, we read about a kind of proto-casemate wall, where those cells are actually houses: "Then [Rahab] let them down by a rope through the window, for her house was on the city wall; she dwelt on the wall" (v. 15). Poorer residents of a city could build their houses against the city wall, saving themselves the effort and cost of building their own fourth wall. The downside, naturally, was that those people became the first line of defense against invaders. Or in Rahab's case, the best informants.

Have you ever noticed that in the Bible, events occur "in" the city gate and not "at" the gate? Now that we know how thick city walls were, it makes sense that no swinging iron or wooden door, as we have them today, would secure a city. Gates would often have four to six chambers, with half the rooms on one side of a passageway and half on the other side. In those chambers the men of the city would meet to decide civic matters. It was in a city gate that Boaz won his right to marry Ruth:

> Now Boaz went up to the gate and sat down there; and behold, the close relative of whom Boaz had spoken came by. So Boaz said, "Come aside, friend, sit down here." So he came aside and sat down. And he took ten men of the elders of the city, and said, "Sit down here." So they sat down...
>
> And all the people who were at the gate, and the elders, said, "We are witnesses. The LORD make the woman who is coming to your house like Rachel and Leah, the two who built the house of Israel; and may you prosper in Ephrathah and be famous in Bethlehem. May your house be like the house of Perez, whom Tamar bore to Judah, because of the offspring which the Lord will give you from this young woman" (Ruth 4:1-2,11-12).

Adjacent to the gate would be the town square, where merchants would sell their produce and products. It was important that the corridor between the chambers of a gate be wide enough to allow cargo inside but narrow enough to keep the gate defensible. To accommodate both, designers of Hazor, Megiddo, Gezer, and other contemporary cities incorporated a right turn within the gate. This would leave potential invaders, who would have carried their shields in their left hands, vulnerable to attack from inside the city.[8]

Residential Dwellings

Knowledge of the typical Israelite's floorplan is surprisingly helpful in understanding stories such as Rahab's. In general, houses were two stories. At least half of the first floor would have been the family's stable, where animals were kept at night so their body heat could warm the upstairs on cool nights. The other half would have been the kitchen. Upstairs would have been a multifunctional space for eating, weaving, and sleeping, although the family might sleep on the roof during hot summer nights. And if the house backed up to a casemate wall, that space between the city's inner and outer wall would likely have been accessible as the family's storage room.[9]

WOMEN'S CLUB

I've heard that there's a fifth Indiana Jones movie in the works (may it be penance for *The Kingdom of the Crystal Skull*!). As long as Harrison Ford keeps coming back for the title role, I will keep spending my money at the box office; but as the last installment introduced Indy's son, I would not be surprised if a new Indiana Jones is introduced soon.

I imagine finding Ford's replacement will be akin to the frequent search for the next James Bond, blond or otherwise. Are there certain physical characteristics to consider? Age, race, hair color, accent? You know that each fan will have an opinion.

If the producers want to be more historically accurate, then they will cast Indiana as a woman. No kidding. Biblical archaeology is a field that has been dominated by women since its inception. No one can tell me why, but archaeology has no glass ceiling.

Arguably the most influential of all archaeologists, Dame Kathleen Kenyon, introduced the strata-dating method to Israel during her work in Jerusalem and Jericho just after World War II. My personal favorite, Trude Dothan (whom I had the great honor of meeting ever-so-briefly in 2004), did a lot of her work on Philistine sites in Israel. Working in Jerusalem today is Eilat Mazar, who makes more popular headlines than almost any other biblical archaeologist as her team regularly uncovers new details of the Israelite monarchy underneath the City of David.

These great women and all other archaeologists, in their own searches for Israelite artifacts, may not have cracked many whips, but I can guarantee they all held on to their brimmed hats.

Arguably the most famous "house" in the Bible is the so-called inn where Mary and Joseph were turned away the night Jesus was born. As a child I always pictured a Tudor-looking structure with Geoffrey Chaucer slamming the front door and leaving the family drenched in pouring rain. None of that is correct.

Archaeology helps us understand what Luke meant when he described Jesus' birth in one short verse, as opposed to how subsequent translations and traditions colored his meaning: "And she brought forth her firstborn Son, and wrapped Him in swaddling cloths, and laid Him in a manger, because there was no room for them in the inn" (Luke 2:7). That one verse, plus the following account of the shepherds and angels out in the fields, give us the basis for our Christmas manger scenes.

The one I grew up with was a wooden barn with Spanish moss "hay" hot-glued everywhere and plastic figurines of the holy family, animals, and the wise men (they are only in Matthew's version, not Luke's). We would then set it up on a fake-snow-covered table in the living room. My parents still have the manger set, and I can—at this moment—smell the thirty-five-year-old moss and wood. How it has survived longer than Jesus walked on earth is a near miracle in itself.

Take a look at two words in Luke 2:7 that give English speakers the wrong impression of what happened that night: *phatne* (translated "manger") and *katalyma* (translated "inn"). Neither is technically mistranslated as far as denotation, but they give us the wrong connotation of the items. Let's start with the inn.

To be more precise, and far less elegant in translation, it is best to read "lodging place" where the NKJV has "inn" because we can't be entirely sure what Luke is describing. Yes, Bethlehem would have had an inn for travelers, and yes, it is entirely reasonable that it was full because every single descendent of King David was visiting that city to complete the nation's census (Luke 2:1-5). Let's stop right there.

If Luke means *katalyma* in the sense of a traditional inn, then he expects his readers to fill in the gap in the story between the No Vacancy sign on the inn and the manger where Jesus took His first nap with knowledge of first-century Jewish hospitality. In Bethlehem and the rest of Judaea, Jews were obligated by their faith to welcome guests no matter the circumstances. They could follow the example of the widow in Zarephath who had fed the traveling prophet Elijah with what she had thought would be her family's last meal (1 Kings 17:8-16). No Jew ever turned away a visitor.

Because it was so common that strangers would lodge a night with any family along their route, Luke may not have been describing an inn at all. It is entirely plausible that Mary and Joseph went straight to a family's home and asked to stay there. There may simply have been no room in the upper part of the house where, you'll remember, beds were laid and food was eaten. (The same word, *katalyma*, also describes this type of second-floor space.) So Mary and Joseph were never turned away from an inn; they just had to stay on the first floor, where the animals and their mangers were kept.

There is no doubt that the word translated "manger" literally means an animal's feeding trough, and while it is uncomfortable to imagine the Savior of humanity sleeping in a dog bowl instead of a lace-covered basinet, His first bed is actually a nod to the hospitality of the Jewish culture and the flexibility of His parents. There were no angry screaming innkeepers turning the family away, no one was prejudiced against an unmarried pregnant woman, and Jesus was born in a house—not a barn. Luke only mentioned the manger because he wanted to contrast the humility of Jesus' birth with the greatness of His Person, not to make us feel sorry for the family. We can lose sight of that important contrast when we misunderstand a culture and fill ourselves with righteous indignation on behalf of people we incorrectly label as persecuted.

Political Life

Not all history is found in physical archaeological artifacts. The nonscriptural writings of people such as the Maccabees and Josephus can be a huge help in understanding the culture and climate into which Jesus was born and lived.

In the section of the Bible called the Deuterocanon (which Catholics accept as Scripture but Protestants and Jews do not) are the four books of the Maccabees. The first book tells the history of the Jews from 175 to 134 BCE. During those years, a powerful family known as the Hasmoneans revolted against the Roman Empire and defeated them in 165. They reconsecrated the temple (which had been converted for the worship of the Greek gods, complete with a Zeus statue and pig sacrifices), instituted Hanukkah, founded a Jewish dynasty, and struggled to rule Judaea for almost a century.

As Judaea descended into civil war, Rome took the opportunity to reacquire the nation as a client state of the empire. By 4 BCE, Rome threw their support behind Herod, the last Hasmonean, and named him king of Judaea. As a puppet of the Roman Empire prone to personal excess and despotic cruelty, Herod watched over the continuing decline of the Jewish state until he died. In 70 CE, Rome would fully reconquer Judaea and utterly destroy the temple.

Between 66 and 73 CE, the Jews revolted against their Roman rulers in the First Jewish War. A future writer named Josephus was a member of the Jewish priestly nobility in Galilee, and he commanded the city's forces against Rome. After his troops were quickly defeated by then-general Vespasian, Josephus essentially defected to the Roman side. He told Vespasian that the Hebrew prophecies foretold the general would be crowned as emperor of Rome, so Vespasian kept him around as an interpreter and slave. Once Josephus's own "prophecy" came true, the new emperor freed him, made him a Roman citizen, and commissioned him to write "factual" accounts of the Jewish Wars, although they were riddled with propaganda supporting the Romans' rule in Judaea.[10]

These events were the backdrop to Jesus' life and the impetus for the founding of various Jewish factions that appear in the Gospels.

Pharisees and Sadducees

Possibly the most famous but least understood of the Jewish sects were the Pharisees. There is no scholarly agreement on who they were, what they believed, or what exactly they did. The most historians can agree upon is that they were reformers who wanted the world to run according to God's will. They seem to have highly valued purity (which made them a bit unsociable outside of their own circle), but they were very politically active. Often they were Roman-government-employed liaisons with the Jews who did what they could to help their own people, but the Pharisees also had a reputation for seizing power from whomever they could.[11]

The Bible often describes the Pharisees as being at odds with the Sadducees, almost as if they were less-musical versions of the Jets and the Sharks from *West Side Story*. When Paul encountered both groups simultaneously as he was on trial for his life in Jerusalem, he cleverly pitted them against each other:

> When Paul perceived that one part were Sadducees and the other Pharisees, he cried out in the council, "Men and brethren, I am a Pharisee, the son of a Pharisee; concerning the hope and resurrection of the dead I am being judged!"
>
> And when he had said this, a dissension arose between the Pharisees and the Sadducees; and the assembly was divided. For Sadducees say that there is no resurrection—and no angel or spirit; but the Pharisees confess both (Acts 23:6-8).

That's about as much as we know about the Sadducees from the Bible: they didn't believe anyone would be resurrected. Josephus tells us a bit more—saying they believed in free will over fate—but the most we can really glean from him is that they were a group of men with shared unknown-to-us beliefs about their faith who tended to be wealthy and were close to the high priest.[12]

Zealots

In the first century CE, in the wake of the Maccabean Revolt, the Romans were still struggling to retain Judaea as part of the empire. A group of lower-class Jews in and around Jerusalem formed into multiple militant political parties that together were known as Zealots. They actively resisted Roman census and taxation, often claiming their religion as the foundation of the movement. Josephus described them this way:

> This school agrees in all other respects with the opinions of the Pharisees, except that they have a passion for

liberty that is almost unconquerable, since they are convinced that God alone is their leader and master. They
think little of submitting to death in unusual forms and
permitting vengeance to fall on kinsmen and friends if
only they may avoid calling any man master.[13]

Such political turmoil is the backdrop of the Gospels. The unrest
among members of the Jewish community makes Jesus' comments
such as, "Render to Caesar the things that are Caesar's, and to God
the things that are God's" (Mark 12:17), controversial.

Jesus tended to speak with members of the lower classes, and
He chose most of His apostles from among them. It is not difficult to assume when those twelve men dropped everything to follow Jesus, they truly believed He was the *Messiah* in the traditional
Jewish sense of the term. All Jews expected that their Savior would
be a literal king who would free His people from the pagan invaders, and in the first century CE, those invaders were the Romans.
Zealots were ready to do anything to have that king crowned. They
were armed and angry with the status quo that left Jews paying fees
to Rome while Rome corrupted their culture with Greek traditions
such as gymnasiums (remember—men played and bathed naked
there), destroyed their temple (70 CE), and seized families' hered-
itary lands.

Some theologians, in the struggle to make sense of Judas Iscariot's last name, have identified him as a Zealot. *Iscariot*, in some texts
of Matthew, seems to be a variant of a Greek word that means "dag-
ger man" or "assassin," both of which would be associated with a
militant revolutionary.[14] Judas is not explicitly called a Zealot in the
Gospels, but Simon is in Luke 6:15, proving that this political fer-
vor was at least known to Jesus and shared by some of His apostles.
Judas's betrayal of Jesus seems logical and almost sympathetic if you

see him this way—as a politically motivated man who knew he had found the Christ and was anxious for Jesus to declare Himself to the world. In this case he is not a villain but a dedicated Jew trying to usher in the new king and found a Jewish state. He didn't betray Jesus for the money, and he killed himself when Jesus allowed Himself to be turned over to Pilate for trial instead of claiming His throne:

> Then Judas, His betrayer, seeing that He had been condemned, was remorseful and brought back the thirty pieces of silver to the chief priests and elders, saying, "I have sinned by betraying innocent blood."
>
> And they said, "What is that to us? You see to it!"
>
> Then he threw down the pieces of silver in the temple and departed, and went and hanged himself.
>
> But the chief priests took the silver pieces and said, "It is not lawful to put them into the treasury, because they are the price of blood." And they consulted together and bought with them the potter's field, to bury strangers in. Therefore that field has been called the Field of Blood to this day.
>
> Then was fulfilled what was spoken by Jeremiah the prophet, saying, "And they took the thirty pieces of silver, the value of Him who was priced, whom they of the children of Israel priced, and gave them for the potter's field, as the LORD directed me" (Matthew 27:3-10).

Don't get me wrong: Judas's actions may have had a historical justification, but they don't make him any less culpable for his sins than the Israelites were for casting the golden calf.

Understanding what was happening in the world when Scripture was enacted and written brings new shades of meaning and interest. Archaeology and nonscriptural texts may correct misinterpretations (such as the questionable presence of a barn in our Christmas manger scenes), but they should never detract from Scripture's truth and God's goal of reconciling humanity to Himself. The knowledge we gain from secular study is at best a tool that may illuminate what God has already given to us in the Bible.

Questions for Discussion and Reflection

1. Descriptions in the Old and New Testaments can be unintelligible to the modern reader who has never seen objects like those described in the text. In your mind's eye, what biblical stories have you staged with modern interpretations of ancient words?

2. Every year archaeological digs uncover artifacts that can have minor and major impacts on biblical interpretation. How can these finds change your view of the ancient world and your understanding of the Bible? Are they helpful?

Chapter 5

KING ARTHUR'S
MANY AUTHORS

Right after my junior prom, everyone who had ridden in our limousine went over to my date's house for an after-party. Our moms were all there, ready with snacks and sleeping bags so we could crash for the night. We were "good kids." At least half the people in that room went on to be valedictorians, and I think we all went to the same church.

With plates full of junk food, hair still stiff with hair spray, and coed appropriate pajamas on our tired bodies, we all settled in front of the television to watch *Monty Python and the Holy Grail*. It was my fault, really. I'd made the mistake of telling some of the guys that I'd never seen it. They were going to educate me that night! As you might guess, I was passed out cold on the hardwood floor twenty minutes later. I just don't enjoy Monty Python movies.

(Six years later some grad-school buddies would try it again: "You watched the wrong one! You'll LOVE *Life of Brian*." No, no I don't.)

Maybe part of the reason I can't get behind *Holy Grail* is that I really do enjoy the more dramatic versions of the Arthurian legends.

Sean Connery is the perfect king in *First Knight*, David and I had our first binge-watching experience with the British television show *Merlin*, and my board-game-loving husband pulls out *Shadows over Camelot* whenever our god-family or brother-in-law is here. Those versions are all about heroism and fantasy and love—not imaginary horses and a killer bunny rabbit.

The Welsh monk Geoffrey of Monmouth gave us the basis of the Arthurian legends in his 1133 book *History of the Kings of Britain*, supposedly based on ancient Celtic historical documents he owned. Over the next fifty-or-so years, French poets would add the stories of the Round Table, the quest for the Holy Grail, and the concept of chivalry to the legend. In 1470 Sir Thomas Malory combined all the known storylines into his book *Le Morte d'Arthur*, which is the foundation for most of our Arthurian imaginings today.[1]

What Malory did with the texts in front of him is called *redaction*. Used in a scholarly and not a top-secret-FBI-files kind of sense, *redaction* is an almost-artistic version of editing that considers all sources, determines who got what right and who got what wrong, and produces a coherent final version of a manuscript. When done well, a redacted manuscript such as Malory's stands the test of time because the final version contains the truths and spirits of all the parts that formed it.

Documentary Hypothesis of the Torah

After finishing a class in the spring of 2004, Dr. Baruch J. Schwartz grabbed four or five other grad students and me as we were leaving the lecture hall. He had been planning a workshop for the following Thursday night and invited us all to attend.

Professor Schwartz was a visiting professor from Hebrew University that semester. I was taking his course "Israel's Prophets as

Messengers of God," but we would soon learn that he had a tangential interest in the origins of Scripture.

Ten of us arrived at Andover Hall that evening. It was a small interior room with no windows and no air conditioning, dark wainscoting that crept three-quarters of the way up the wall, and a giant solid-wood table that left barely enough room for chairs. Professor Schwartz was already in there handing out papers with Scripture fragments from Exodus printed all over them. At the top of each page was a letter: *J*, *E*, or *P*. "You've all learned about the Documentary Hypothesis, haven't you?"

WHEN A *J* IS REALLY A *Y*

Have you ever noticed that some words beginning with *j* are pronounced as if they begin with a *y*? Words that have come into the English language directly from languages such as German, Dutch, and Swedish sometimes retain their native pronunciation of the letter *j*. For example, *Johannesburg* is pronounced YO-hahn-is-burg, not JOE-hahn-is-burg.

This piece of usually useless trivia is surprisingly helpful when studying theology. Take the Divine Name, which English speakers transliterate as *Yahweh*. Germans transliterate it as *Jahweh* because in their language *j* sounds like *y* (and incidentally, their *w*s sound like *v*s). Because Germany was the home of Protestant thought and the country continues to be a center for biblical scholarship, they influence the world's theological terminology. That's how we end up calling the Yahwist source the "J source"—because in German, it is the Jahwist source.

A more popular example of this phenomenon is in the word *Jehovah*. The word is a transliterated translational nightmare! Its story began when a German transliterated the consonants of God's name (remember, there were no vowels in early Hebrew) to JHWH. Although we've pretty much always known which vowels go between those consonants thanks to the Greek version of the Hebrew Bible, some Christians in the thirteenth century decided to make a change. They took the vowels from *adonai* (the Hebrew word for "lord") and crammed them between JHWH. That's Ja-ho-vah, which we English speakers then mispronounce as Juh-ho-vuh and spell *Jehovah*.

As I said: transliterated translational nightmare!

In 1885 a German biblical scholar named Julius Wellhausen wrote a series of articles describing the four sources or "people" who recorded the oral traditions that would become known collectively as the Torah. He named them Yahwist (J), Elohist (E), Priestly (P), and Deuteronomist (D). Each source is unique in its style, theme, vocabulary, and even chronology, but all were put together by later redactors to give us the Bible we have today.

- The Yahwist, so named because he uses the Divine Name *Yahweh* throughout his writings, was probably the first of the four sources. He writes in a narrative style that is the basic framework for the Torah upon which the other sources build.

- The Elohist, so named because he calls God *Elohim* instead of using the Divine Name, is also a narrative writer. His work shows an interest in divine revelations, likes to explore humanity's experiences with sin, guilt, and innocence, and emphasizes the "fear of God" whenever possible.

- The Priestly source, so named because he is more concerned with what would concern priests—right worship of God and purity of the individual—than with narration, is the primary author of Leviticus and Genesis 1.

- The Deuteronomist, so named because he wrote most of Deuteronomy, recorded his words just after the destruction of Jerusalem in 586 BCE. He is also responsible for the books of Joshua, Judges, and Samuel–Kings, and his narrative arc demonstrates a desire for his contemporary exiles to recognize how Israel's past sin led to Babylon's conquest of them.

According to the Documentary Hypothesis, all four sources are found in each book of the Torah, but scholarship differs on the details of who recorded exactly what and how much. As we discussed in chapter 1, Moses originated the material in oral tradition, but the Documentary Hypothesis states that others recorded his words hundreds of years later. They acted as his ghostwriters, if you will. He originated the material as tradition affirms, but he probably wasn't the guy who sat down and put pen to parchment. Note that this explanation of the Torah's development is a *hypothesis* and not a *theory*, meaning it is still being tested and debated.

The Mt. Sinai Expeditions

"Tonight you are going to redact the Bible the way the first scribes did." Professor Schwartz had us begin by reading Exodus 19 aloud. "Stop whenever something sounds like it is being repeated," he told us.

> In the third month after the children of Israel had gone out of the land of Egypt, on the same day, they **came to the Wilderness of Sinai.** For they had departed from Rephidim, **had come to the Wilderness of Sinai, and**

camped in the wilderness. So Israel **camped there
before the mountain** (emphasis added).

We stopped after the first two verses. We marked our Bibles at
that point, then continued the exercise for the rest of the chapter. We realized that over the three days described in Exodus 19,
Moses went up and down Mt. Sinai four times. Today, experienced
hikers on well-worn paths can go from the base to the 7,497-foot-
elevation summit in about three hours (so that's six hours round
trip). Assuming Moses was super-fit and God blazed a path for him
on an otherwise-remote mountain, Moses was actively hiking at
least twenty-four out of ninety-six hours to an elevation well above
Denver's. That seems a bit unrealistic, doesn't it?

"Take a look at the papers in front of you. Each one represents
what I believe the complete texts of the J, E, and P sources looked
like before redactors put them together. If you were editing the final
version of the Torah—and you believed that all sources are divinely
inspired—how would you put them together?"

We all agreed: "Wherever the sources say the same thing, write
it down once. Wherever the sources disagree, include both versions.
Delete nothing." We did just that with the J, E, and P sources, and
we ended up writing *exactly* what is in Exodus 19.

At the end of the evening, Professor Schwartz explained why he
had done this exercise with us. "I am a theologian who believes in
the Bible while working for secular institutions. Most Bible scholars who accept the Documentary Hypothesis use it to prove that
the Bible is not divinely inspired but is the work of people. I see
the opposite. I see that four different versions of the Torah existed,
and when the scribes sat down to combine them, they made no
choices and no changes to any of them because all four were divinely
inspired—as were the scribes themselves."[2]

The Creation Stories

The seeming contradictions or impossibilities in Scripture are often evidence of the scribal work to blend the four sources of the Bible together. The most glaringly obvious evidence of multiple scriptural sources is right at the start of the Bible in the creation accounts.

The Bible opens with God stoically commanding everything into existence from afar in Genesis 1:1–2:3. This story stands apart from the rest of Genesis. The account has a strong internal structure that is almost poetic, as God declares every part of creation "good" and each day is summed up as "the evening and the morning." Like His creation, that description has order. The second version of God's creation is in Genesis 2:4–3:24. It is the narrative story of creation with characters, actions, and emotions.

Scholars who specialize in the field of source criticism declare that each story has a different origin: Genesis 1 was recorded by P, while Genesis 2–3 is the work of J.[3] I can imagine the scribes sitting in a room, as we did, with both complete manuscripts of the stories. They look at them both and discuss, what's the same? What parts of these two stories can be harmonized to give us the one perfect version of creation? The answer was, nothing.

Since the scribes knew that both were God-inspired, they included both in their entirety. No editing or blending. No decision-making. So Genesis 1 ordered creation as (1) plants, (2) animals, and then (3) humanity, while Genesis 2–3 ordered it as (1) man, (2) plants, (3) animals, and then (4) woman. It had to be God, because no good editor would have allowed himself to keep those contradictions in any text, let alone a sacred one.

Consider our impression of God and His creation if all we had was P's story—the first one. We would know that we are created in

God's image, but we might have no idea what that means. He gave us one giant command:

> "Be fruitful and multiply; fill the earth and subdue it; have dominion over the fish of the sea, over the birds of the air, and over every living thing that moves on the earth."

> And God said, "See, I have given you every herb that yields seed which is on the face of all the earth, and every tree whose fruit yields seed; to you it shall be for food. Also, to every beast of the earth, to every bird of the air, and to everything that creeps on the earth, in which there is life, I have given every green herb for food" (Genesis 1:28-30).

Those instructions are not very detailed; P doesn't bother to record *how* we are supposed to make more and subdue everything. We seem to be on our own, the final creation of a distant, grand Power who made the universe, made us to take care of it, then left on holiday.

In J's version, we meet God as a person. He seems like any other dad who enjoys long walks in the park on cool days (Genesis 3:8) and asks questions to which He already knows the answers: "Who told you that you were naked? Have you eaten from the tree of which I commanded you that you should not eat?" (3:11). He punishes misbehavior, but He cares for Adam's and Eve's physical and emotional needs throughout that punishment by clothing their now-embarrassing nakedness (3:21).

We need the details that come in both stories. Without Genesis 1, we would not know that we have been created "in God's image," and those three words actually foreshadow the events of J's story, in which humanity tries to elevate themselves from being like God to being gods themselves. (In truth, that is humanity's MO through-out the whole Bible.) J also answers that *how* question that P left hanging: How are we supposed to care for God's creation?

- tend and keep the garden (2:15)
- name (that's ancient Hebrew shorthand for "take owner-ship of") the living creatures (2:19)
- marry (2:24)
- bring forth children physically (3:16)—not speaking them into creation
- till the ground (3:23)

If God seems cold in P's version just after He makes humanity on day six, then J explains why: the entrance of sin into God's cre-ation. God created perfection, and humanity went and ruined it. They forced Him into a fix-it mode that would require laws and sacrifices, the death of His one perfect Son, and eventually the return of His Son to get the earth back to where He'd made it in the first place. We simply can't imagine that level of cosmic frus-tration, and maybe that's why He needed two different sources to convey it all to us.

Two-Source Hypothesis of the Gospels

As a conservative Jew, Professor Schwartz didn't have any interest in the development of the Gospels, but plenty of people do. When I was in undergrad, I was first exposed to the Two-Source Hypoth-esis in a course called "Jesus in History."

The idea behind this hypothesis is a lot like the one that prompted the Documentary Hypothesis: There were two original written sources on Jesus' life. Matthew and Luke had access to both, but they wrote their own books independently of each other. What do we call these sources? The Gospel of Mark and *Q*. Yes, we have another seemingly bizarre name to thank the Germans for. The *Q* stands for *Quelle*, which is the German word for "source."

Why Mark?

The Gospel of Mark is believed to be the oldest of the four Gospels and is certainly the most basic. It's a You-Are-There kind of account of Jesus' life: no fancy words, no apparent agenda. It's pretty much just the facts. It opens with John the Baptist announcing the beginning of Jesus' ministry, wasting no time on His birth or childhood. It ends with the women leaving the empty tomb with a message for the rest of the disciples: He is risen! Mark isn't particularly concerned with the following proliferation of Jesus' message or the development and growth of the church. He is writing about Jesus, and that is all.

Tradition holds that John Mark, Paul's companion on many missionary journeys, was the author. Modern scholars believe that is unlikely and just consider the author to be anonymous. This person was, however, a likely firsthand or close secondhand witness of the events of Jesus' life, and he finished his work before Rome destroyed the Jewish temple in 70 CE. His close proximity to his subject in space and time makes this Gospel particularly reliable and a good candidate for—I'll just say it—*plagiarism* by Matthew and Luke. Good thing there was no Roman copyrighting back in the first century!

Who was Q?

When you put Matthew, Mark, and Luke side-by-side, it is easy to highlight what all three have in common. These three books are called the *Synoptic Gospels* for that very reason; they share a lot of the same stories, their timelines are similar, and in places they use the same words and phrasing. What may be surprising is just how much Matthew and Luke line up with each other, to the exclusion of Mark. Scholars believe there must have been a second source that both Matthew and Luke had on their desks for reference. This hypothetical source would have been mainly a listing of Jesus' quotations—as if an ancient reporter had been following Him around everywhere with a tiny spiral notebook and a pencil behind his ear. If Q ever existed, then it is a shame we no longer have a copy. It would have been by far the oldest of the gospel accounts and would have had the best recollection of Jesus' words.[4]

Some New Testament scholars have reverse-engineered the Q source (the way Professor Schwartz reverse engineered J, E, and P's versions of Exodus 19 for us), using the commonalities in Matthew and Luke as their raw material.[*] When the entire source is by itself, it looks something like this...

Q 6:20-21 *The Beatitudes for the Poor, Hungry, and Mourning*

[20]And [[rais]]ing his [[eyes to]] his disciples he said: Blessed are [[«you»]] poor, for God's reign is for [[you]]. [21]Blessed are [[«you»]] who hunger, for [[you]] will eat [[your]] fill. Blessed are [[«you»]] who [[mourn]], for [[<you>will be consoled]].

Q 6:22-23 *The Beatitude for the Persecuted*

[22]Blessed are you when they insult and [[persecute]] you, and [[say every kind of]] evil [[against]] you because of the son of man. [23]Be glad and [[exult]], for vast is

---

your recompense in heaven. For this is how they [[per-secuted]] the prophets who «were» before you.

Q 6:?24–26? The Woes

?24?«But woe to you that are rich, for you have received your consolation.» ?25?«Woe to you that are full now, for you shall hunger. Woe to you that laugh now, for you shall mourn and weep.» ?26?«Woe to you, when all men speak well of you, for so their fathers did to the false prophets.»

Q 6:27-28, 35c-d Love Your Enemies

27Love your enemies 28[[and]] pray for those [[perse-cuting]] you, 35c-dso that you may become sons of your Father, for he raises his sun on bad and [[good and rains on the just and unjust]].

Q 6:29-30 Renouncing One's Own Rights

29[[The one who slaps]] you on the cheek, offer [[him]] the other as well; and [[to the person wanting to take you to court and get]] your shirt, [[turn over to him]] the coat as well. Q/Matt 5:41[[«And the one who conscripts you for one mile, go with him a second.»]] 30To the one who asks of you, give; and [[from the one who borrows, do not [[ask]] back [[«what is»]] yours.

Q 6:31 The Golden Rule

31And the way you want people to treat you, that is how you treat them.

Q 6:32, 34 Impartial Love

32..If you love those loving you, what reward do you have? Do not even tax collectors do the same? 34And if you [[lend «to those» from whom you hope to receive, what <reward do>you < have>]]? Do not even [[the Gentiles]] do the same?

Q 6:36 Being Full of Pity like Your Father

[36] Be merciful, just as your Father .. is merciful.

Q 6:37-38 Not Judging

[37]..Do not pass judgment, «so» you are not judged. [[For with what judgment you pass judgment, you will be judged.]] [38][[And]] with the measurement you use to measure out, it will be measured back to you.[5]

Any scholars who initially resisted the idea of a sayings source backpedaled when a nearly complete copy of the noncanonical Gospel of Thomas was discovered in 1945. That gospel is line after line of direct quotes, each beginning with "Jesus said" or "He said." Occasionally the disciples are quoted, too, but there is no narrative tying the quotes together—no context, if you will. The Gospel of Thomas simply demonstrates that "sayings gospels" existed as a genre, making the Q source more probable.

How did Matthew and Luke do it?

Based on their final products, it seems that Matthew and Luke each had a culture-motivated goal when writing his Gospel. Matthew's version is very Jewish. His additions to the work of Mark and Q are often concerned with showing how Jesus fulfilled the Jews' expectations for a Messiah. For example, His birth narrative has a genealogy that goes back to Abraham, the father of God's people. He records how Jesus becomes an exile in Egypt when a wicked king declares the genocide of young boys, which is reminiscent of Moses and the Exodus. And He is descended from King David through His adoptive father, Joseph. Matthew wants none of his Jewish readers to doubt that Jesus was the Jewish Messiah. He just includes that perspective when relating Mark's rather strict history and Q's direct quotations.

Luke knew he would have a different set of readers—non-Jewish Christians. As a companion to Paul, he traveled the Roman Empire to churches in many nations. For him, Jesus is not just the Jews' Messiah but everyone's Christ. He traces Jesus' heritage all the way back to Adam to solidify this point, and he is much more concerned with Jesus' treatment of the poor and outcasts of society than he is with Hebrew prophecies. He also goes on to record the development of the early church in the book of Acts. That narrative book has no antecedents as do Matthew and Luke, but it does give context for many of the Epistles that follow it.

THE CHRIST

Throughout this book, you will notice that I tend to refer to Jesus as "the Christ" and not just "Christ." That is not a typo.

The word *Christ* is not an English word; it is also not a translation of anything. It is a *transliteration* from Greek into English. Someone took the English letters that sound like their Greek counterparts in *Christ* and recorded those in Scripture instead of translating them. This is a common practice in two instances: for names that do not have translations, and for words we can't precisely translate. In the New Testament the words *deacon, baptize, apostle,* and *angel* are all also transliterations of Greek words; they have no inherent English meanings.

Too many people think of *Christ* as Jesus' last name, maybe because it is transliterated in the same way that *Jesus* is. But *Christ* is a unique title that means "anointed one." When the New Testament writers were calling Jesus "Christ," they were translating the Hebrew word *messiah* (which also means "anointed one") into Greek. This would have been obvious to most of their first-century readers, but it is too often lost on modern English readers because we don't translate the Greek, we only transliterate it.

Like most questionable translation choices in our versions of the Bible, *Christ* was retained because of tradition. Today people tend to get very upset when you mess with that word in any context. How many times have you heard that the shorthand *Xmas* "takes Christ out of Christmas"? That's incorrect. The *X* is not an English letter but the Greek letter *chi*, which is one of the original Christian symbols for Christ. (It's like the cross, only it's based on language instead of an ancient Roman torture device. The *X* came to symbolize Christ at least a century before the cross did!)[6]

When The Voice Bible translation was released by Thomas Nelson in 2012, the media—secular and religious—had a field day. This was the first English Bible version to actually translate almost every word in the New Testament. *Angel* became "messenger"; *apostle* became "emissary"; *baptize* became "immerse." News organizations sensationalized what was really a nonstory with headlines like "The Voice Takes 'Christ' Out of the Bible." Sometimes the articles would go on to explain the truth behind the sensational headline—that the version translates *Christ* into its English meaning of "Anointed One" instead of just transliterating the word from the Greek—but very few people bothered to read beyond the bold letters at the top of the page. A tool that could have enlightened many Christians to the true meaning of *Christ* was lost to the work of attention-grabbing writers and lazy readers.

That event is why I often put *the* in front of *Christ*. When you read

that word, I don't want you to think of it as a last name but as the
righteous and unique title it actually is.

Both Matthew and Luke were inspired by God to write their
Gospels. Just as both P's and J's accounts of creation are necessary
to see different facets of God, both of these books demonstrate the
different but equally important truths that the Christ died for Jews
and He died for Gentiles. The Jews needed to recognize His sacrifice as the fulfillment of God's promises, and the Gentiles needed to
learn how Jesus' death adopted them into Abraham's family. Thanks
to divine inspiration, there's a book for each of those.

What About John?

We've analyzed three Gospels, yet we haven't mentioned the
fourth Gospel even once. Poor John. His work tends to be ignored
as scholars rip into each other attempting to explain who wrote what
first, when, and why. That's because the Gospel of John stands alone.
It was written later, doesn't seem to rely on any other texts, and has
a completely different structure and purpose.

John's Gospel—maybe because it was finished several decades
after all the others—is much more detailed and a bit more symbolic.
Jesus' ministry lasts three years for John, but only one year for the so-
called Synoptic Gospels of Matthew, Mark, and Luke. And those
three years are filled with stories unmentioned by the other writers, such as Jesus curing the blind man at the pool of Siloam (John
9) and raising Lazarus of Bethany from the dead (John 11). Jesus'
speeches are significantly longer, as John remembers them, and the
crucifixion time-line is totally different. The Synoptics say that Jesus'
Last Supper was the Passover meal, but according to John, Jesus was
crucified and buried before Passover begins making Him the Passover Lamb. If you find yourself newly confused every Holy Week

about exactly what happened on which day, this is the reason for it and you're not alone.

So the Gospel of John doesn't need a hypothesis. His work comes from one source—himself—and stands alone, giving us details of Jesus' ministries and words that the others don't include and emphasizing the symbolic nature of Jesus' life and work.

After-the-Fact Sources of Mark

Remember when I wrote that Mark ends with the women leaving the empty tomb (Mark 16:8)? Did you think, *That's not right. My Bible says that Jesus "was received up into heaven, and sat down at the right hand of God. And [the disciples] went out and preached everywhere, the Lord working with them and confirming the word through the accompanying signs"* (verses 19-20). My Bible says that too. But if your Bible translation is worth the paper it's printed on, you'll have a footnote following verse 8 that says something like, "Verses 9-20 are not in the original text. They are lacking in Codex Sinaiticus and Codex Vaticanus, although nearly all other mss. of Mark contain them."

The truth is that Mark ended his Gospel at verse 8. Several hundred years later, Christians who were dissatisfied with his abrupt conclusion decided to create their own endings. Redacted in those last twenty-two verses are four distinct sources—none of which match the original author of Mark. Take a look:

(The bold section is from Matthew, italics are from Luke, and underlined is from John; the regular Roman font is the final redactor.)

> Now when He rose early on the first day of the week, **He appeared first to Mary Magdalene, from whom He had cast out seven demons.** She went and told those who had been with Him, as they mourned and wept.

And when they heard that He was alive and had been seen by her, they would not believe it.

After that He appeared in another form to two of them as they walked into the country. And they went and told it the rest, but they did not believe them either.

Later He appeared to the eleven as they sat at the table; and He rebuked their unbelief and hardness of heart, because they did not believe those who had seen Him after He had risen. And He said to them, <u>"Go into all the world and preach the gospel to every creature. He who believes and is baptized will be saved; but he who does not believe will be condemned.</u> And these signs will follow those who believe: In My name they will cast out demons; they will speak with new tongues; they will take up serpents; and if they drink anything deadly, it will by no means hurt them; they will lay hands on the sick, and they will recover."

So then, after the Lord had spoken to them, He was received up into heaven, and sat down at the right hand of God. And they went out and preached everywhere, the Lord working with *them* and confirming the word through the accompanying signs.

To state the truth about the end of Mark is not heretical or sacrilegious, but it is antitraditional (which, sadly, some people consider tantamount to heresy). The Greek used in these verses is much more polished than anything Mark wrote, and the simple inclusion of passages from John's Gospel is a dead giveaway that this ending isn't original because the Gospel of Mark was completed about fifty years before the Gospel of John was. There is no doubt that the ending was a later fabrication; the earliest Christian theologians had never read it: "Clement of Alexandria [c. 150– c. 210] and Origen [c. 184– c. 253] show no knowledge of the existence of these verses; furthermore Eusebius [c. 260– c. 340] and Jerome [347–420] attest that the passage was absent from almost all Greek copies of Mark known to them."[7] Each of those men is a church father. What they said and wrote was foundational for Christianity as we know it.

Later redactors of Mark probably added the final verses because they thought Mark should seem more like the other three Gospels. The popularity and not the originality of the *epilogue*, if you will, led to it being included in the Latin translation of Scripture (called the Vulgate), which was used for all subsequent Catholic translations of the New Testament and the King James Version of Mark.[8] Because the endings were part of the Vulgate, all were included in the official Christian canon.

But why isn't Mark's epilogue fully incorporated with the rest of the Gospel while other redacted portions of the Bible are well integrated into the books in which they appear? It isn't easy to separate J, P, E, and D sources from one another, but the four endings of Mark get special typesetting and explanatory footnotes in most Bible translations! The differences mostly come down to timing.

When the redactors of the Torah and the Synoptic Gospels were doing their work, they were part of the books' creation processes. Scripture was not considered the God-breathed final version until their work was done. In the case of Mark, Christian fathers such as Clement, Origen, Eusebius, and Jerome obviously accepted Mark's Gospel with its original ending as Scripture hundreds of years before redactors made their changes, and over one thousand years before the New Testament was canonized. By the time the New Testament canon was closed in 1546, the developmental history of Mark was known, so Bible translators and printers retained that history in the anthologies we read today.

The authors of the books of the Bible are not as easy to identify as we may think. Is the Torah Moses' brainchild? I would say yes, but in the sense that he started the oral traditions that many other scribes, writers, and redactors molded—according to God's inspiration—into the Scripture we have today. All the little things that don't make sense on the surface, such as the existence of two creation stories, are really there because God wanted them left alone.

The existence of Mark's epilogue proves this. Several hundred years after Mark was finished writing, other men sat down and "fixed" the Gospel of Mark to make it fit better with the other Gospels. They didn't do a great job, and that's why we can easily recognize the changes today. But it occurs to me that maybe their C-level work is part of God's plan. For without it, we might not have recognized how God inspired many sources and more editors to produce His final perfect Word. There is method in that madness.

Questions for Discussion and Reflection

1. It is comfortable to envision one author sitting down and writing a book of the Bible from beginning to end—no interruptions, no help from the audience—but the oldest manuscripts and original languages seem to indicate that is an unlikely scenario. How would the involvement of more than just one person in the development of the books of the Bible and its subsequent translations change your understanding of how God gave us His Word?

2. Secular theologians love to point out the apparent contradictions in the biblical text as evidence that God's Word is not inspired, but many Jewish and Christian

theologians use the same "errors" as evidence that God did inspire the writers and editors who finalized the books. Do the source hypotheses for the Old and New Testaments answer any questions you may have about the biblical text?

Chapter 6

SEEING CINDERELLA'S
SLIPPER CLEARLY

When I was growing up, I loved watching the television channel AMC. Back in the 1990s, they actually played "American movie classics" all the time and without commercial interruption. The only original programs were the introductions Nick Clooney would film for the start of each movie. If you're a fan of PBS's *Masterpiece* today, then it was a lot like Laura Linney reminding us where we left our friends last week on *Downton Abbey* or Alan Cumming introducing us to an uninterrupted hour of *Sherlock*.

On the weekends, AMC would often play marathons of the Rodgers and Hammerstein films that had been adapted from their Broadway musicals or written directly for the screen. I recorded most of them on VHS tapes so I could watch again and again and memorize the songs. My absolute favorite was *Cinderella*. Rodgers and Hammerstein's *Cinderella* has the distinction of being the only musical they wrote just for television. The original version starring Julie Andrews debuted in 1957, but I loved the 1965 version with Leslie Ann Warren in the title role.

David had no idea what he was starting when he told me that a touring company was bringing a stage version of Rodgers and Hammerstein's *Cinderella* to our local theatre. He bought us two tickets as my Christmas present, and he endured my listening to the old film—now digital files on my tablet instead of my long-since-lost homemade VHS tapes—again and again until the night of the production.

When David purchased the tickets, he noticed a disclaimer: "This is not Disney's *Cinderella*. Songs, characters, and scenes may differ." That was not news to me, but I guess I'm in the minority. When we got to the theatre, the same message was posted all over the place with the added line, "NO REFUNDS." Apparently people had been demanding their money back when their children were unable to sing along with the musical.

When we sat down inside the sold-out theatre, David and I noticed two fiftyish women sitting behind us. They were talking a little loudly and sloshing their double-pours of red wine in plastic cups before the show began. One was telling the other just how much she loved this musical. But her tune changed by intermission: "This is *not* how the story goes! Cinderella is supposed to lose her shoe at the ball, and the fairy godmother is not a crazy homeless woman!" She vented for the next ten minutes, then continued pointing out what she thought to be mistakes in the production until it ended. They managed to follow us out of the theatre, too, and I heard her say, "We should ask for our money back!" just as we walked past the NO REFUNDS sign.

What is the "right" version of the Cinderella story? Is it Disney's 1950 cartoon? If so, then why isn't it frame-for-frame identical to their own 2015 live-action remake? Was Drew Barrymore's *Ever After* right to make Leonardo da Vinci into the "fairy godmother"? Why do all three television versions of Rodgers and Hammerstein's musical look and sound totally different from the stage production they inspired? And where on earth do ABC's *Once Upon a Time* Cinderellas—Ashley and Jacinda—fit in this mess?

Is there not one original manuscript of the Cinderella story that everyone can agree is perfect? I would have guessed that the Grimm brothers' version of Cinderella was the original—sawed-off stepsister toe and all[1]—but I would have been very wrong. Similar stories date as far back as 4 BCE and have distinct versions in cultures all over Asia and Europe.[2] The truth is that there is no existing original Cinderella story, just all the bits and pieces that produced the versions we know and love (or loathe, in the case of our tipsy theatre friend) today.

Lost in Translation

"Some claim the shoe was made of fur. Others insist it was glass. Well, I guess we'll never know."[3] So said the German Wilhelm Grimm to the French Danielle de Barbarac's great-great-granddaughter in an American film with a Scottish actor playing the prince. It is this pan-European character that makes *Ever After* my favorite film version of the Cinderella story. (Sorry, Disney.)

In the opening scene, the Grimm brothers make a good point about the fairy tale: by the time they wrote it down more than a century after the actual events (that is, the film's fictional version of "actual events"), the translation of the story from village to village and then one nation to another had irreversibly changed it. The only way to know what the shoe looked like was to go back to the source—Cinderella's own family.

This can happen to all kinds of manuscripts, even scriptural ones, over place and time. We have no original manuscripts of any books in the Bible—and obviously all of the original actors are long dead by now—so we are stuck trying to figure out "what the slipper was made of" with either an "old" Greek translation from around 200 BCE (called the Septuagint) or a "new" Hebrew transcription from the 900s CE (called the Masoretic text). This begs the question, is more lost in translation or in a millennium?

WHAT IS THE SEPTUAGINT (AND WHY SHOULD I CARE)?

Around 250 BCE, King Ptolemy II of Egypt wanted to have a copy of every book in the world translated into Greek and placed in his library. So his royal librarian wrote a letter to Eleazar, the high priest in Jerusalem, asking that he assemble six elders from each of the twelve tribes of Israel and send them to Alexandria with the Torah. Upon arrival, all seventy-two were individually cloistered in the then-new, now-ancient-wonder Lighthouse at Alexandria for seventy-two days. When the men emerged, each had produced exactly the same translation as the other men there—seventy-two identical but individual translations! They read the translation to the Egyptian Jews and the court. Ptolemy was so impressed that he sent the men back to Jerusalem with gifts for themselves and their high priest, Eleazar.

Like most legends, there's probably a bit of truth somewhere in that fantastic story. The Septuagint, a word that derives from the Latin word for "seventy," was indeed a miraculous document because of what it did, if not how it developed. About one hundred years before it was translated, Alexander the Great had conquered Israel, Egypt, and the rest of the Mediterranean nations, so everyone's official language was changing to Greek, no matter where he lived or whom she worshipped. Many Jews in and out of Israel no longer spoke their ancestral language of

Hebrew, so the Septuagint was crucial in bringing the Hebrew Scriptures to Jews and non-Jews throughout the Roman Empire.

The Septuagint was also crucial to the development of the early Christian church. It was obviously in use by Jesus and the apostles because its versions of Hebrew Scriptures are quoted roughly three hundred times all over the New Testament.

We should be thankful the Septuagint arrived when it did because it laid the groundwork for Jesus' mission to bring all nations—not just the Jews—into His Father's family. It may not be word-for-word perfect, but its creation by Jews in a pagan nation for use by everyone in their known world mirrors God's redemptive work and indicates the translation process was God-inspired.

In this section, the "slipper" we are trying to identify is the name of the sea that God separated for the Israelites in Exodus 14:26-29:

> Then the LORD said to Moses, "Stretch out your hand over the sea, that the waters may come back upon the Egyptians, on their chariots, and on their horsemen." And Moses stretched out his hand over the sea; and when the morning appeared, the sea returned to its full depth, while the Egyptians were fleeing into it. So the LORD overthrew the Egyptians in the midst of the sea. Then the waters returned and covered the chariots, the horsemen, and all the army of Pharaoh that came into the sea after them. Not so much as one of them remained. But the children of Israel had walked on dry land in the midst of the sea, and the waters were a wall to them on their right hand and on their left.

In this prose description of events, notice that the body of water is simply called "the sea." There is no proper name for it.

The following chapter, Exodus 15, is a poem known as the "Song of the Sea." It's a nominee for the Oldest Part of the Bible Award along with the "Song of Deborah" (Judges 5:2-31). It praises God for saving the Israelites from the Egyptians and then goes on to describe how other Israelite enemies such as the Canaanites and Philistines were terrified by His strength:

> Pharaoh's chariots and his army He has cast into the sea;
> His chosen captains also are drowned in the **Red Sea**.
> The depths have covered them;
> They sank to the bottom like a stone.
>
> Your right hand, O Lord, has become glorious in
>   power;
> Your right hand, O Lord, has dashed the enemy in
>   pieces.
> And in the greatness of Your excellence
> You have overthrown those who rose against You;
> You sent forth Your wrath;
> It consumed them like stubble.
> And with the blast of Your nostrils
> The waters were gathered together;
> The floods stood upright like a heap;
> The depths congealed in the heart of the sea.
> The enemy said, "I will pursue,
> I will overtake,
> I will divide the spoil;
> My desire shall be satisfied on them.
> I will draw my sword,
> My hand shall destroy them."
> You blew with Your wind,

The sea covered them;
They sank like lead in the mighty waters.
(Exodus 15:4-10, emphasis added)

On the surface, it seems that the older source of the story knows exactly where it happened: at the Red Sea. It is the younger prose description that lacks detail. But your Bible translation is deceiving you unless it includes a footnote on verse 4 that reads something like "Lit. *Sea of Reeds*." (If your Bible doesn't have that footnote, I strongly suggest you find and read one that does.)

In the Hebrew, the words that our Bibles tend to render as "Red Sea" are *yam suph*. *Yam* means "sea." No problem there. But *suph* is a little trickier. Let's start by saying what it is not: "red." The word we would translate as "red" is *adam*, as in that guy named Adam whom God created from rich red-colored dirt and whose skin can be reddened by the sun. Obviously this is a common word that would have been known to Moses as he composed the Song of the Sea, so if he had meant "Red Sea," then I think he would have sung it. And if somehow Moses had gotten it wrong in the original version, then the generations of people who sang *yam suph* for hundreds of years would have changed it, or the scribes who finally wrote the song down would have corrected it. And if all those people missed the "error," then so did every other Bible character who ever mentioned the event! Check out Joshua 24:6; Deuteronomy 11:4; Psalm 106:7,9,22; Psalm 136:13-15; and Nehemiah 9:9. Those all say *yam suph*, too, not *yam adam*.

So why have Bible translators knowingly wrongly translated *yam suph* for so long? Tradition.

The first translation of the Hebrew Bible—and oldest complete manuscript in any language by about one thousand years—is the Greek translation called the Septuagint. It made the first attempt to "correct" what presumably had been written in the even older Hebrew manuscripts we no longer have today. It replaced what we would call an improper noun and adjective, *yam suph*, with a proper noun, Red Sea, presumably in an attempt to help readers more quickly understand where the actions were taking place. This is a common translational practice. I can promise you there are tons of places where your Bible reads, "Jesus said" or "Paul said" or "Methuselah said," but the Greek or Hebrew originals just have "he said." In a string of he-saids, he-saids, he-saids, adding the antecedent is helpful and often necessary.

Other translations then followed the Septuagint's lead without really questioning whether the addition was correct. The Latin translation did it in 400 CE, the King James Version did it in 1611, and almost all modern translations in all languages have followed suit. The one exception on my bookshelf is the Jewish Study Bible, and that's because it doesn't use the Septuagint as its basis for English translation of this phrase as do all the others I own.

It is impossible to know exactly why the translators of the Septuagint decided to edit the Hebrew, but the best idea I've heard is that *yam suph* is used in other places in the Bible where other geographical details make it clear that those writers were referring to the Red Sea, as we call it today. For example, "King Solomon also built a fleet of ships at Ezion Geber, which is near Elath on the shore of the *yam suph*, in the land of Edom" (1 Kings 9:26). There is little doubt that this passage is talking about our Red Sea based on the three other locations mentioned. But the problem is, we can't assume that *yam suph* always means the Red Sea. It would be like assuming *highway* always refers to Route 66 or *ice cream* always means Baskin-Robbins's World Class Chocolate (if only it did!).

So if it doesn't mean "red," then what does *suph* mean? Most scholars today will tell you it comes to Hebrew from an Egyptian word that means "reed." *Yam suph* translates to "reed sea" and describes a shallow body of water where papyrus reeds can grow. A lot of researchers really like this idea because it makes God's dividing of the sea physically possible and not necessarily miraculous: a strong wind would be enough to carve a path in a papyrus marsh. (Of course it is difficult to then imagine an entire army drowning in the same papyrus marsh, but those researchers tend to ignore that problem with their interpretations.)

But isn't it odd that passages such as 1 Kings 9:26, which very obviously is referring to the Red Sea, would describe that body of water as a sea of reeds when it has always been too deep and too salty to grow papyrus on its shores? Of course it is. You might as well call *frozen yogurt* "ice cream"!

Allow me to suggest that we don't actually understand what the ancient writers meant by *suph*. In 1984 a religious studies professor suggested to *Biblical Archaeology Review* readers that *suph* might not be an Egyptian loan word meaning "reed," but may in fact be related to the Hebrew word *soph*, meaning "end."[4] This results in *yam suph* meaning something like "sea at the end [of the world]." In that case, the improper noun *yam suph* could describe any large body of water where a distant shore could not be seen or had not been discovered. In the ancient Near East, this could have described the Red Sea, the Mediterranean Sea, the Black Sea, or even the Persian Gulf.

The "end" translation never caught on in theological circles, but its sheer reasonableness reminds me that no one knows everything when it comes to Scripture. Even simple solutions to big problems such as *yam suph* can be overlooked when thousands of years of tradition have so trained us to believe what may or may not be correct. Today, thanks to two separate traditions, we have the people who believe wholeheartedly that God split the Red Sea only because that's what King James said. We also have the people who scoff at the Red Sea tradition and say God (or no one) let a medium-sized wind or tide move about twelve inches of water somewhere along the Nile River. Might I suggest they both may be wrong?

My mother-in-law likes to say, "When we all get to heaven, we will all know that we were all wrong." As the Grimm brothers would never learn the "original" story of Cinderella, we probably won't ever know what body of water God parted. This may, in fact, be by design. God doesn't want us to spend our lives trying to track down every movement of the Exodus only to hang our faiths on what *we* find based on *our* translations. He wants us to recognize how mighty and loving He is—so loving that He would alter His own creation for a day to protect His people.

Blurred Vision

In the stage version of Rodgers and Hammerstein's *Cinderella* that David and I watched, one of the (not-so-terribly) wicked stepsisters, Charlotte, is both figuratively and literally nearsighted. She is so self-involved that she misses much of what is happening around her, and she wears the thickest glasses you've ever seen. (She was by far my favorite character—not so sickeningly sweet as Cinderella can sometimes be.) I have been similarly myopic since I was eight years old, so I know how disconcerting it is to wonder if you can trust what your eyes are telling you.

It is a known phenomenon in the book industry that you see more mistakes when editing on paper than you do on a computer screen. Most publishing houses I've worked for are going completely paperless, and while it has its advantages (such as cost and speed), it is very hard on my eyes. They are the only things I more diligently protect from the sun than my so-white-it's-really-blue skin, but even with UV- and blue-light-blocking coatings on my sunglasses and reading glasses, a simple bright light can keep me from seeing clearly. Just staring at a computer screen too long can bring on a migraine.

I am thankful today that most of the time I'm reading and typing in English. When I was in college and grad school, each annual eye exam showed my vision worsening. It wasn't my age or even the amount of time I spent on the computer. It was the hours and hours I stared at Hebrew; it was almost literally blinding.

Which is easier to see, the Hebrew or English version of Psalm 23:1? I'm not asking you to read either, but to consider the details that your brain must recognize:

אֶחְסָר: לֹא רֹעִי יְהוָה   The LORD is my shepherd;
                                    I shall not want.

The Latin alphabet is a lot easier on the eyes, isn't it?

Now imagine you're reading handwritten—not perfectly typed—Hebrew characters in a world where artificial light has not yet been invented. And you're trying to copy every curve, line, and dot to perfection because those letters form the Word of God. Would you get a headache? Probably. Might you make a mistake? Almost definitely.

The academic community has all kinds of fancy terms for when scribes made a copying mistake, but they all boil down to a scribe mis-seeing something. Without the benefit of ancient autocorrect, those mistakes became part of Scripture's history, and each discrepancy between manuscripts needs to be evaluated to determine which version is more likely the correct representation of the original. That's how you end up with scholars sometimes disagreeing about what the Bible says: because manuscripts say different things. It's a he-wrote, he-wrote.

Let's think about these copying mistakes in terms of common vision problems:

Astigmatism

When you have astigmatism (as I do), the letters on a doctor's eye chart are blurry no matter how close or far away you are standing. No amount of squinting helps in my case; a *P* could just as easily be an *F* or *D*. Would misreading the *P* have a big impact on the meaning of a sentence? What do you think:

> The woman ate her pill.
>
> The woman ate her fill.
>
> The woman ate her dill.

Each of those sentences is grammatically correct and has a distinct meaning. One or two may be more likely than the others, and context could certainly help us know if the woman was sick, stuffed, or just a big fan of pickles.

A word in 2 Kings 20:4 probably suffered from someone's "astigmatism." Your Bible reads something such as, "And it happened, before Isaiah had gone out into the middle *court*, that the word of the Lord came to him" (emphasis added). But the Hebrew literally reads, "before Isaiah had gone out into the middle *city*." A scribe misread חצר for העיר. See how close they are? Thankfully the context of the passage makes it pretty obvious that Isaiah went to the middle of the court, so don't be too alarmed if your Bible didn't footnote that one for you.

Blinking

You might not have astigmatism or any of the other conditions we are about to discuss, but I bet you blink. It's one of those lovely involuntary reflexes (such as breathing) that God gave us. If you are a contact lens wearer, you are all the more aware of how restorative blinking can be.

But blinking does force you to unfocus and refocus your eyes. Think about when you're reading a recipe. Do you ever lose your place? If you've just put in one tablespoon of sugar, when you glance back to your place, might your eyes mistakenly land on one tablespoon salt instead, causing you to miss an ingredient and ruin the food? I've done it; I think we all have.

It is pretty likely that the scribe copying the Hebrew text of David and Goliath's battle made a similar mistake. In 1 Samuel 17:4, Goliath is described as "six cubits and a span." All good Sunday school kids know this translates to a remarkable nine feet four inches tall. What a giant! The thing is, that is probably a scribal error. Look at verse 7: "his iron spearhead weighed six hundred shekels." Might the copyist have seen the "six" as he glanced from scroll to scroll and accidentally copied that number instead of a more reasonable smaller number? This isn't really a hypothetical question. In the Septuagint (which is a translation but is also a millennium closer to the original text than the Hebrew versions we have), Goliath's height is "four cubits and a span," which is about six feet and six inches. That is still incredibly tall by modern and especially ancient standards, so the meaning of the passage is unaffected. But its plausibility does increase.

Dyslexia

Have you ever transposed letters or numbers? Back when we all used to take messages on paper and write down telephone numbers, I was the world's worst for inverting digits. Now that my smartphone logs numbers and names, I rarely do that anymore. But take a look at my text messages. Not two hours ago I messaged my husband, "Do you want me to lay out some *stakes* for tonight?"

I promise: we aren't planning to go vampire hunting on this lovely Thursday evening. We just want to grill some beef tenderloin.

There is a fair amount of letter swapping in the Bible too. In Deuteronomy 31:1, Moses "went and spoke these words to all Israel." Except that he may have "finished speaking these words to Israel." In the first quote, which is probably in your Bible, the Masoretic text uses a form of the verb *ylk*, which means "to go," and naturally the past-tense verb form translates to "went." Moses "*went* and spoke." The Dead Sea Scrolls, which preserve an older version of the Hebrew than the Masoretic text does, use a form of the verb *ykl*, which means "to finish," so Moses "*finished* speaking." Whatever manuscript the Septuagint translators were following also used *ykl*, so that likely is closer to the original writer's word.

Hallucination

I was so excited last year when it was time for David to get his eyes checked. For the past year, we'd noticed that I was able to read street signs and billboards better than he could (with the aid of my contact lenses, naturally). *Finally*, I thought, *he can stop bragging about his 20-10 vision!*

What happened at the optometrist might have been even better than I'd hoped, if my only goal was to tease him mercilessly. David's vision is still better than perfect, but as the doctor explained to him, his brain gets ahead of his eyes and makes him see words that are not there.

"So you hallucinate?" I asked.

"Pretty much."

Obviously this type of hallucination is much milder than what we imagine when we hear the word *hallucinate*. When I woke up from a total hysterectomy with zero pain medicine left in my system, the agony caused me to hallucinate for six solid hours. Thankfully we are here to talk about David's kind of mostly harmless hallucinations, not my visions of horrific things.

In 2 Samuel 15:7, Absalom is planning to take Israel's throne from his father, King David. The writer tells us, "Now it came to pass after *forty* years that Absalom said to the king, 'Please, let me go to Hebron and pay the vow which I made to the LORD'" (emphasis added). Whether the text means *forty years* literally or in the figurative sense of "generation" as we discussed in chapter 2, the time line does not work. Considering that King David only ruled a total of forty years or one generation (1 Kings 2:11), the scribe accidentally added the Hebrew equivalent of a zero onto the end of the word *four*.

In almost all manuscripts of 2 Samuel, with the exception of the Masoretic text, which has been translated here, Absalom planned his rebellion for *four* years.

Double Vision

Remember in the old Looney Toons when Wile E. Coyote would accidently blow himself up or stand under his own falling anvil? He would look up, see two, three, even four images of the Roadrunner wavering before his eyes, and shake his head before—meep meep!—they ran off as one. That's double vision. I've only had it once when, like an idiot, I stumbled over the edge of the bathtub while painting the wall, fell backward, and hit my head on the lip of the shower stall. I wish the two paint rollers I remember seeing could have finished that job twice as fast!

There's some double vision in the Bible too. Leviticus 20:10 tells us, "The man who commits adultery with another man's wife, he who commits adultery with his neighbor's wife, the adulterer and the adulteress, shall surely be put to death." (Just imagine if society followed that rule today! But I digress...)

A more literal translation looks something like this:

A man who commits adultery with the wife of

a man who commits adultery with the wife of
his neighbor:
in that case the adulterer and adulteress shall be put to death.

Unless Leviticus was being put to music (and I can pretty much promise a law like this *was not*), then there isn't a great explanation for the repeated line except scribal error. It isn't a big deal—the worst the error does is give a Motown feel to the reading of the law—but it is there.

What I have just described is called a *doublet*, and there are a lot of them in the Bible. Some of them are quite long, most famously the Wife-Sister Narratives in Genesis, where that law from Leviticus is remarkably pertinent. There are three of these "doublets," so technically they constitute a *triplet*. Although categorized in the same way as the scribal duplication in Leviticus 20:10, the similarities in the three Wife-Sister Narratives did not develop from a copyist misreading a manuscript but from earlier writers using the same story structure three separate times. If these stories were on prime-time television, they would be "procedurals" that always have the same format but different guest stars interacting with the principal actors each week.

In these stories Abraham and Isaac try to pass their wives off as their sisters because they are afraid of being killed by foreign men who want to marry their beautiful wives. Presumably Abraham and Isaac thought the Egyptians and Philistines would find murder preferable to adultery.

In the first story, Abram is basically a pimp. Harsh, but true. He pretends that Sarai is his sister so that the Egyptians won't kill him and take her, but she ends up going to live with Pharaoh while Abram is showered with expensive gifts that sound suspiciously like the payment of a bride price:

Now there was a famine in the land, and Abram went down to Egypt to dwell there, for the famine was severe in the land. And it came to pass, when he was close to entering Egypt, that he said to Sarai his wife, "Indeed I know that you are a woman of beautiful countenance. Therefore it will happen, when the Egyptians see you, that they will say, 'This is his wife'; and they will kill me, but they will let you live. Please say you are my sister, that it may be well with me for your sake, and that I may live because of you."

So it was, when Abram came into Egypt, that the Egyptians saw the woman, that she was very beautiful. The princes of Pharaoh also saw her and commended her to Pharaoh. And the woman was taken to Pharaoh's house. He treated Abram well for her sake. He had sheep, oxen, male donkeys, male and female servants, female donkeys, and camels.

But the LORD plagued Pharaoh and his house with great plagues because of Sarai, Abram's wife. And Pharaoh called Abram and said, "What is this you have done to me? Why did you not tell me that she was your wife? Why did you say, 'She is my sister'? I might have taken her as my wife. Now therefore, here is your wife; take her and go your way." So Pharaoh commanded his men concerning him; and they sent him away, with his wife and all that he had (Genesis 12:10-20).

Except for the messy detail that Abram and Sarai were married, this would have been a common marriage contract. Pharaoh gave all the gifts to Abram as the bride price to "buy" Sarai. It is not clear if "taken to Pharaoh's house" means she was part of his harem or became a wife of royal standing, but either way, the implication is that they slept together. The fact that God sent plagues underscores this possibility since adultery would have been Pharaoh's only crime, until he lied about it, that is.

One time wasn't enough for old Abraham (and by now he was old). After he left Egypt—and after he made his covenant with God (Genesis 17)—Abraham pulled the same con and married Sarah off to the king of Gerar:

> And Abraham journeyed from there to the South, and dwelt between Kadesh and Shur, and stayed in Gerar. Now Abraham said of Sarah his wife, "She is my sister." And Abimelech king of Gerar sent and took Sarah.
>
> But God came to Abimelech in a dream by night, and said to him, "Indeed you are a dead man because of the woman whom you have taken, for she is a man's wife."
>
> But Abimelech had not come near her; and he said, "Lord, will You slay a righteous nation also? Did he not say to me, 'She is my sister'? And she, even she herself said, 'He is my brother.' In the integrity of my heart and innocence of my hands I have done this."
>
> And God said to him in a dream, "Yes, I know that you did this in the integrity of your heart. For I also withheld you from sinning against Me; therefore I did not let you touch her. Now therefore, restore the man's wife; for he is a prophet, and he will pray for you and you shall live. But if you do not restore her, know that you shall surely die, you and all who are yours."
>
> So Abimelech rose early in the morning, called all his servants, and told all these things in their hearing; and the men were very much afraid. And Abimelech called Abraham and said to him, "What have you done to us?

How have I offended you, that you have brought on me and on my kingdom a great sin? You have done deeds to me that ought not to be done."...

So Abraham prayed to God; and God healed Abimelech, his wife, and his female servants. Then they bore children; for the Lord had closed up all the wombs of the house of Abimelech because of Sarah, Abraham's wife (Genesis 20:1-9,17-18).

All signs point to Abimelech and Sarah consummating their marriage. He "took" Sarah (the Hebrew word has that connotation), he paid Abraham for her, he gave them part of his land to live on as he would family, he paid twenty times the highest bride price to "vindicate" Sarah "before everybody," and God had "closed up all the wombs of the house of Abimelech because of Sarah" as if her womb needed protecting. But the story says Abimelech "had not come near her," and God agrees.

This is one of those I-don't-know instances when we can't understand the text. But it is worth noticing that Abimelech's wives weren't the only ones whose wombs God opened. In the next chapter, Sarah is pregnant with her son.

Isaac must have heard those stories of his parents, because he did exactly the same thing with his wife, Rebekah, also in Gerar with a king named Abimelech (who may or may not have been the same man who married Sarah):

So Isaac dwelt in Gerar. And the men of the place asked about his wife. And he said, "She is my sister"; for he was afraid to say, "She is my wife," because he thought, "lest the men of the place kill me for Rebekah, because she is beautiful to behold." Now it came to pass, when he had been there a long time, that Abimelech king of the Philistines looked through a window, and saw, and there was Isaac, showing endearment to Rebekah his wife. Then Abimelech called Isaac and said, "Quite obviously she is your wife; so how could you say, 'She is my sister'?"

Isaac said to him, "Because I said, 'Lest I die on account of her.'"

And Abimelech said, "What is this you have done to us? One of the people might soon have lain with your wife, and you would have brought guilt on us." So Abimelech charged all his people, saying, "He who touches this man or his wife shall surely be put to death" (Genesis 26:6-11).

If this is the same Abimelech, then he had certainly learned his lesson about marrying the sisters of refugees in his country. Isaac told the same lie, but Rebekah was spared Sarah's fate.

The stories themselves don't have much moral value, except maybe to remind men not to lie about their relationships with their wives, but they do have redemptive value. These people were all liars and possibly adulterers. In the short term, God saved them from the situations they brought upon themselves and rewarded them with wealthy lives. In the long term, Abraham, Sarah, and Isaac managed to make it into the so-called Hall of Faith:

By faith Abraham obeyed when he was called to go out to the place which he would receive as an inheritance. And he went out, not knowing where he was going. By faith he dwelt in the land of promise as in a foreign country, dwelling in tents with Isaac and Jacob, the heirs with him of the same promise; for he waited for the city which has foundations, whose builder and maker is God.

> By faith Sarah herself also received strength to conceive
> seed, and she bore a child when she was past the age,
> because she judged Him faithful who had promised.
> Therefore from one man, and him as good as dead, were
> born as many as the stars of the sky in multitude—innu-
> merable as the sand which is by the seashore (Hebrews
> 11:8-12).

They are among the Old Testament's greatest heroes, in spite of what they deliberately did wrong. That is a fact all us sinners should celebrate—in triplicate.

～∕ ⌒∕

As the books of the Bible passed from generation to generation and group to group, errors in translation and handwriting produced multiple manuscripts that aren't always identical to each other. Although it might be easier to study the Bible if—like the fabled seventy-two copies of the Septuagint—every manuscript were identical, that isn't reality.

The real shame is not the existence of the manuscripts' differences but the ways some people use them to "prove" the Bible is not God's inspired Word. I and many Bible-believing scholars like me see just the opposite in the Bible's so-called mistakes. If Christians are aware of how their Bible translations developed and what textual imperfections are being addressed in them, then they are less likely to have their faiths shaken by any "gotcha" statements of nonbelievers. None of the manuscripts' differences matter to the gospel message of the Bible; they simply provide a little color for people like me who enjoy using their latent OCD for the powers of good and analyzing the anomalies to death.

No one ever knows the exact origin of any story. Details can get lost to oral traditions and failing memories long before they are obscured by messy handwriting and poor translation. We need to embrace the beauty of Scripture in its current form while acknowledging its long and multicultural past. Because like our local theatre, God doesn't give refunds if we don't like His story.

Questions for Discussion and Reflection

1. There are hundreds if not thousands of biblical manuscripts, many of which are yet to be read or even discovered. When those manuscripts disagree or when the Hebrew or Greek words are ambiguous, do you see errors that nullify or mysteries that color God's Word? Why?

2. The printing press not only sped up the production of Bibles, but it also created standardized translations that were no longer vulnerable to scribal error and that popularized some manuscripts over others. When you learn about contradictions between manuscripts, do you automatically trust the version that is traditional or do you consider the merits of other versions?

Chapter 7

MACBETH AND THE SELF-FULFILLING PROPHECIES

I f you're a fan of the Harry Potter movie franchise, you may remember a brief scene in *The Prisoner of Azkaban* when a choir dressed in black robes and holding giant toads performs the song "Double Trouble" as the students enter the Great Hall for the first time that year.[1] It sets an appropriately ominous tone for the rest of the film. The song is based on a chant of Shakespeare's Weird Sisters in his play *Macbeth*:

> Double, double toil and trouble;
> Fire burn and caldron bubble...
> For a charm of powerful trouble,
> Like a hell-broth boil and bubble.[2]

In the play, the three witches give Macbeth glimpses of the future, first of him becoming king of Scotland and then of his death. For Macbeth, these messages become self-fulfilling prophecies. He murders the current king and then seizes the throne for himself. Because Macbeth becomes a tyrant as he murders more and more people attempting to cover up his first crime, he is later killed by a nobleman who is loyal to the king's son. It seems none of the events of the play would have happened had Macbeth not visited the witches. In the end, the outcome of the king's son ascending the throne was unchanged. The magical prophecies brought nothing but unnecessary death, madness, and destruction.

This commonly happens in literature. Prophecies are much more dangerous when they are spoken aloud than if they had never come to light. If Oedipus had never heard the prophecy of the oracle at Delphi stating he would marry his mother and kill his father, would he have unknowingly left his adoptive home and returned to his birthplace—the only city where he could and would unknowingly do both? And, going back to the Harry Potter series, if Voldemort had not been told that someone born on Harry's birthday would one day kill him, would he have attempted to murder Harry— unintentionally giving him the power to fulfill the prophecy?

Of course self-fulfilling prophecies are not entirely fictional. Have you ever been told to "fake it till you make it" when applying for jobs? The idea is that you may not be qualified to do something now, but once you *must* do it, you figure out how to succeed. That may be a good strategy for your career, but it is not how God intends for us to live our lives. He doesn't want us searching the world for solutions we can effect by ourselves; He wants us listening to Him so He can bring about His will through us. The future is all about Him, not us.

Pagan Divination and Worship

Israel was unique among ancient Near Eastern nations in their devotion to one all-powerful God. Most civilizations believed in dozens or even hundreds of different gods and goddesses who controlled different parts of nature. The Canaanites, whom the descendants of Moses' followers would one day conquer and on whose land the twelve tribes would eventually build their nation, believed in a king of the gods named El. His queen consort was Asherah, and his most famous and popular son was Baal.

Baal was the god of storms, so he controlled the fertility of the land in an area of the world that tends to be arid. Because rain was necessary for life, it is no wonder that the Canaanites worshipped him so intensely—or that their practices were adopted by the Israelites again and again.

Just like Adam and Eve, all humans want to be gods. And if we can't make ourselves into gods by eating from the tree of knowledge or building a tower into heaven, then we like to think we can at least control them. There is no controlling Israel's God—no matter how hard we may pray or how much we may bargain with Him—but it was thought that pagan gods liked to be bribed by their worshippers. The people believed that if they could sacrifice enough, then the god would honor their wills and not his own.

AKHENATEN

It seems there is always an exception to the rule. For about seventeen years, between 1353 and 1336 BCE, Israelites technically weren't the only monotheists in the region. During those years, the Egyptians were commanded by their pharaoh to worship only one god, Aten. Although it is unlikely that most people completely abandoned their religions just because their king told them to do so, Egypt was legally (if not practically) a monotheist nation for those seventeen years.

The pharaoh's name, which he adopted in honor of his one god, was Akhenaten. He spent his reign tearing down temples to the god Amun and chiseling his name and the names of other gods and goddesses out of reliefs. He also built himself a brand new capital at Amarna and a temple dedicated to Aten at Karnak.

All of Akhenaten's changes were reversed when his young son, Tutankhamun, ascended the throne with a team of regents in 1332. The advisors restored the worship of Amun then set about removing all references to Aten and Akhenaten himself throughout Egypt. Thankfully they weren't perfectly successful in their destruction. The new city at Amarna was so quickly abandoned that it survived to become one of the best-preserved archaeological sites in Egypt. Without the advisors' haste, we might not know about the Egyptian monotheist.

In biblical stories, when humans tried to take control of fate, the results were always disastrous. In 2 Kings 3:26-27, Mesha, the king of Moab, sacrificed his own son, the crown prince, to win a battle against the Northern Kingdom of Israel.

> And when the king of Moab saw that the battle was too fierce for him, he took with him seven hundred men who drew swords, to break through to the king of Edom, but they could not. Then he took his eldest son who would have reigned in his place, and offered him as a burnt offering upon the wall; and there was great indignation against Israel. So they departed from him and returned to their own land.

The most disturbing part of this story is that the sacrifice worked. Exactly why it worked has been the subject of speculation for centuries. In Mesha's own account of the war on the Mesha Stele, he argued that Chemosh, god of the Moabites, saw the sacrifice and responded. Others placed the massacre at the feet of Israel's God. Practical scholars would argue that the sacrifice simply inspired his troops to victory. No matter the reason, this human sacrifice resulted in many deaths on both sides of the battlefield and a change to the line of succession in Moab.

It is not, then, surprising that God would literally outlaw all pagan rituals:

> When you come into the land which the LORD your God is giving you, you shall not learn to follow the abominations of those nations. There shall not be found among you anyone who makes his son or his daughter pass through the fire, or one who practices witchcraft, or a soothsayer, or one who interprets omens, or a sorcerer, or one who conjures spells, or a medium, or a spiritist, or one who calls up the dead. For all who do these things are an abomination to the LORD, and because of these abominations the LORD your God drives them out from before you. You shall be blameless before the LORD your God. For these nations which you will dispossess listened to soothsayers and diviners; but as for you, the LORD your God has not appointed such for you (Deuteronomy 18:9-14).

God goes on to say that He will communicate with His people through a new kind of prophet, someone such as Moses who speaks God's words as God tells him to. None of God's prophets would be slaves to the people, giving answers upon request. They would work only for God.

Sadly, not all of the Israelites were satisfied with the limits God put on divination and their own perceived abilities to influence the future. Kings and generals would be some of the worst offenders, and the disastrous effects of their sins are recorded in the Bible. Judges 11 recounts the horrific story of Jephthah, an Israelite judge and general who foolishly offered to sacrifice to God whatever first greeted him when he returned from war if God would grant his wish for victory. He expected an animal, but his daughter ran out to see him instead. Jephthah sacrificed his child in order to settle his bargain with God.

The books of Kings are filled with monarchs from the Northern Kingdom of Israel and the Southern Kingdom of Judah who just couldn't help but honor other nations' gods or worship Israel's God in places other than Jerusalem. I suppose they were following in the footsteps of their renown predecessor, Solomon, who in his last years started worshipping the gods of his foreign wives:

> For it was so, when Solomon was old, that his wives turned his heart after other gods; and his heart was not loyal to the LORD his God, as was the heart of his father David. For Solomon went after Ashtoreth the goddess of the Sidonians, and after Milcom the abomination of the Ammonites. Solomon did evil in the sight of the LORD, and did not fully follow the LORD, as did his father David. Then Solomon built a high place for Chemosh the abomination of Moab, on the hill that is east of Jerusalem, and for Molech the abomination of the people of Ammon. And he did likewise for all his foreign wives, who burned incense and sacrificed to their gods (1 Kings 11:4-8).

God would punish him by tearing Israel apart. Solomon's son would continue to rule the Southern Kingdom, made up of the tribes of Judah and Benjamin, while Solomon's servant Jeroboam would become monarch of the Northern Kingdom that contained the other ten tribes.

Israel's first king, Saul, wasn't a perfect God worshipper either. Just before a battle against the Philistines, Saul consulted a medium.

He had been following God's instructions as long as the prophet Samuel had been there to give him God's messages, but since Samuel's death, Saul was feeling rudderless. (This was, of course, by God's design, since He intended for Saul to lose his war with David.)

> Then Saul said to his servants, "Find me a woman who is a medium, that I may go to her and inquire of her."
>
> And his servants said to him, "In fact, there is a woman who is a medium at En Dor."
>
> So Saul disguised himself and put on other clothes, and he went, and two men with him; and they came to the woman by night. And he said, "Please conduct a séance for me, and bring up for me the one I shall name to you."...
>
> Then the woman said, "Whom shall I bring up for you?"
>
> And he said, "Bring up Samuel for me."...
>
> Now Samuel said to Saul, "Why have you disturbed me by bringing me up?"
>
> And Saul answered, "I am deeply distressed; for the Philistines make war against me, and God has departed from me and does not answer me anymore, neither by prophets nor by dreams. Therefore I have called you, that you may reveal to me what I should do."
>
> Then Samuel said: "So why do you ask me, seeing the LORD has departed from you and has become your enemy? And the LORD has done for Himself as He spoke by me. For the LORD has torn the kingdom out of your hand and given it to your neighbor, David. Because you did not obey the voice of the LORD nor execute His fierce wrath upon Amalek, therefore the LORD has done

this thing to you this day. Moreover the LORD will also deliver Israel with you into the hand of the Philistines. And tomorrow you and your sons will be with me. The LORD will also deliver the army of Israel into the hand of the Philistines" (1 Samuel 28:7-8,11,15-19).

It is possible that Saul thought he'd found a loophole in God's prohibition against divination. Yes, he used a medium—a necromancer, really, whom he himself had recently exiled from Israel—but the king did it in an effort to hear from God through one of His approved prophets, Samuel.

Why was this still a problem for God? Because Saul was trying to get God to bend to his will. He might as well have offered his son Jonathan up to God as an offering, as Mesha offered his son to Chemosh, or made a deal with God in exchange for a sacrifice, as Jephthah did. All these stories prove that God doesn't like it when we try to get Him to share a secret we aren't ready to hear.

God-Sanctioned Prophecy

While the Old Testament was being lived out and written about, God had prophets walking the earth, giving His messages directly to humanity. You've heard of a lot of these guys; most of them even have books named after them. Moses, Samuel, Nathan, Elijah, Jeremiah, and Hosea are just a few of the people God used before Scripture was canonized. Their words eventually became Scripture itself.

Old Testament Prophets

In the Old Testament, most of the recorded prophecies were warnings to the prophets' contemporaries about the coming destruction of the Northern Kingdom of Israel and the Southern Kingdom of Judah. Everyone was being admonished to right worship of God or they were going to die. God was clearly telling everyone how *not* to self-fulfill His prophecies.

In the Northern Kingdom, this was a particularly difficult message. At the core of God's instructions to His worshippers was the necessity to sacrifice to Him only in Jerusalem. Jerusalem was in the Southern Kingdom, and the two parts of Israel were more often enemies than friends. No one was giving day passes so Northerners could travel to Jerusalem to worship. (That would have been interpreted as an invitation to invasion.) Instead, the North had their own temple-ish sites, called *high places*. Those were the biggest problems for Elijah, Elisha, Amos, Hosea, and Nahum.

> And the LORD said to me, "Amos, what do you see?"
> And I said, "A plumb line."
> Then the Lord said:
> "Behold, I am setting a plumb line
> In the midst of My people Israel;
> I will not pass by them anymore.
> The high places of Isaac shall be desolate,
> And the sanctuaries of [the Northern Kingdom of]
>   Israel shall be laid waste.
> I will rise with the sword against the house of
>   Jeroboam" (Amos 7:8-9).

Because the simple existence of these high places was flouting God's law, they were too easily and too often converted from worship of just God to worship of the indigenous gods.

The Northern Kingdom ignored the advice of prophet after prophet until the nation was conquered by the Assyrian Empire in 722 BCE. The conquerors destroyed the cities, moved the Israelites to other parts of the empire, and moved Assyrian citizens into the Northern Kingdom. Because they could not follow God's first command to worship only Him and because they did not listen to right prophecy when God gave it, ten tribes of Israel were "lost" as they blended into the Assyrian Empire.

The Southern Kingdom had the same problem with high places, but they had no excuse for building them other than laziness. High places were built because people wanted to worship God where they lived and not where He lived. They didn't want to make the effort to travel to Jerusalem and do it right, even when King Josiah told them to do so:

> [Josiah] brought all the priests from the cities of Judah, and defiled the high places where the priests had burned incense, from Geba to Beersheba; also he broke down the high places at the gates which were at the entrance of the Gate of Joshua the governor of the city, which were to the left of the city gate. **Nevertheless the priests of the high places did not come up to the altar of the LORD in Jerusalem**, but they ate unleavened bread among their brethren (2 Kings 23:8-9, emphasis added).

Thanks to some reforming kings, including Josiah, the Southern Kingdom managed to stave off their fate until 586 BCE, when the Babylonians burned Jerusalem to the ground and exiled prominent members of society throughout the Babylonian Empire. Attitudes like those of the high-place priests who would rather worship their easy way instead of God's right way could not be amended by God's prophets or kings.

Most of the prophets' words were fulfilled with the falls of the Northern and Southern Kingdoms. God exacted His justice by scattering His people as He promised He would. But He had also promised through His prophets that the Israelites would be able to return to Jerusalem:

"I will take you from among the nations, gather you out of all countries, and bring you into your own land. Then I will sprinkle clean water on you, and you shall be clean; I will cleanse you from all your filthiness and from all your idols. I will give you a new heart and put a new spirit within you; I will take the heart of stone out of your flesh and give you a heart of flesh. I will put My Spirit within you and cause you to walk in My statutes, and you will keep My judgments and do them. Then you shall dwell in the land that I gave to your fathers; you shall be My people, and I will be your God. I will deliver you from all your uncleannesses. I will call for the grain and multiply it, and bring no famine upon you. And I will multiply the fruit of your trees and the increase of your fields, so that you need never again bear the reproach of famine among the nations. Then you will remember your evil ways and your deeds that were not good; and you will loathe yourselves in your own sight, for your iniquities and your abominations. Not for your sake do I do this," says the Lord GOD, "let it be known to you. Be ashamed and confounded for your own ways, O house of Israel!" (Ezekiel 36:24-32).

Such prophecies of a return to Jerusalem would be fulfilled again and again. Ezra and Nehemiah describe how after Persia conquered Babylonia in 539 BCE, their king allowed the Jews to return and helped them rebuild. Then, after Rome conquered Persia in 333 BCE, the Jews won their independence from Rome in 160 BCE—although Judaea would soon be folded back into the empire and become Hellenized. In 70 CE, Rome would burn Jerusalem's temple to the ground. The Jews would not control Israel again until 1949, and they are still waiting to rebuild God's temple.

Apocalypse

Into war-ravaged Israel was born a specific kind of prophecy called *apocalypse*. It is "a genre of revelatory literature with a narrative framework, in which a revelation is mediated by an otherworldly being to a human recipient, disclosing a transcendent reality which is both temporal, insofar as it envisages eschatological salvation, and spatial, insofar as it involved another, supernatural world."[3] In simpler words, an apocalypse is the recording of a supernatural experience that results in a human becoming privy to future events. Each Testament of the Bible contains one apocalypse: Daniel 7–12 in the Old Testament and Revelation in the New Testament.

Daniel 7–12

I like to think of the book of Daniel in two parts. In chapters 1 through 6, we meet Daniel and learn to trust him as a man of God who has been gifted with the ability to interpret dreams. In chapters 7 through 12, Daniel is the one given a dream that requires interpretation.

The format of the book demonstrates the important lesson that one person cannot receive a prophecy in a vacuum, no matter how he or she has been gifted by God. Certainly Daniel might have been capable of interpreting his own dreams as he had the dreams of others, but God sent him a corroborating witness, in the form of a heavenly messenger, for his visions of God's final judgment of the world.

> I, Daniel, was grieved in my spirit within my body, and the visions of my head troubled me. I came near to one of those who stood by, and asked him the truth of all this. So he told me and made known to me the interpretation of these things: "Those great beasts, which are four, are four kings which arise out of the earth. But the saints of the Most High shall receive the kingdom,

and possess the kingdom forever, even forever and ever"
(Daniel 7:15-18).

As a unit, Daniel's dreams describe how God will destroy the
wicked empires of the world that have persecuted His people. The
prophecies have already been fulfilled several times in the rise and
fall of the ancient Near Eastern empires of Babylon, Persia, and
Greece, but they remain relevant today. God's people may have
changed from just the Jews to all the Jesus followers, but the strug-
gles of righteous people against oppressive regimes will not end until
the prophecy is fulfilled one last time with the return of Jesus.

Such important prophecies must be tested. In Deuteronomy,
God tells the Israelites how to distinguish true from false prophecies:

> And if you say in your heart, "How shall we know
> the word which the LORD has not spoken?"—when a
> prophet speaks in the name of the LORD, if the thing
> does not happen or come to pass, that is the thing which
> the LORD has not spoken; the prophet has spoken it pre-
> sumptuously; you shall not be afraid of him (Deuteron-
> omy 18:21-22).

Prophecy is serious stuff. The person speaking it must cite God
as the source of the message, and the message must come true.

Paul would elaborate on these proofs as he spread Jesus' gospel message because the gift of prophecy was especially important
to first-century Christians. Without the New Testament Scriptures,
all revelations came to them as God-inspired words from the apostles. The first criteria, much like Deuteronomy's insistence that the
prophecy must be from God, was that the prophet must confess
Jesus as Lord: "Now concerning spiritual gifts, brethren, I do not
want you to be ignorant: You know that you were Gentiles, carried
away to these dumb idols, however you were led. Therefore I make

known to you that no one speaking by the Spirit of God calls Jesus accursed, and no one can say that Jesus is Lord except by the Holy Spirit" (1 Corinthians 12:1-3).[4]

The apostle John also elaborated on how a true prophet could be distinguished from a false one, and he highlighted the importance of doing so:

> Beloved, do not believe every spirit, but test the spirits, whether they are of God; because many false prophets have gone out into the world. By this you know the Spirit of God: Every spirit that confesses that Jesus Christ has come in the flesh is of God, and every spirit that does not confess that Jesus Christ has come in the flesh is not of God. And this is the spirit of the Antichrist, which you have heard was coming, and is now already in the world.
>
> You are of God, little children, and have overcome them, because He who is in you is greater than he who is in the world. [The false prophets] are of the world. Therefore they speak as of the world, and the world hears them. We are of God. He who knows God hears us; he who is not of God does not hear us. By this we know the spirit of truth and the spirit of error (1 John 4:1-6, antecedent added).

Like Daniel, John would receive an apocalyptic message of his own. And like Daniel, he had a thorough understanding of how prophecy should be interpreted before his own dream.

Revelation to John

Revelation has all the hallmarks of good entertainment: fantastic creatures, an ethereal setting, war between good and evil, and a promise of a better future. It was probably the first book of the Bible I read completely as a child (I did not understand a word!), and it was the first book David's and my small group wanted to study back when Nathan was a part of it. That also makes it the first book of the Bible I had to—and I use this word loosely—teach.

Volumes of books have been written about how to interpret Revelation, and I feel as if I've read them all. Scholars have spent their careers developing theories about how and when the events have already or will one day happen. On a lot of churches' unwritten and unspoken "applications" for membership, you have to decide if you are a preterist, historicist, futurist, or spiritualist; and you better say the right thing or you're out of their club!

I can promise you one thing: No one has ever entirely understood Jesus' Revelation, and no one will until He returns. He said so: "But of that day and hour [when heaven and earth will pass away] no one knows, not even the angels in heaven, nor the Son, but only the Father. Take heed, watch and pray; for you do not know when the time is" (Mark 13:32-33). When the time comes, the fulfillment of the prophecy will be obvious to those who know God and are living just to achieve His one will of humanity's reconciliation with Him.

So what does Revelation itself tell us, and how does the book fit with the rest of the Bible? In his dream, John visits God's heavenly throne room as Jesus is preparing to return to earth and finally remove the sin Adam and Eve and all of us found to be so tasty. He watches as the world is destroyed by natural and supernatural disasters, as two beasts, a dragon, and the dead receive final judgments, and as a new heaven and earth are born. God comes to live with His people on this new earth where sin does not exist, as He intended to do before creation.

The Bible's last word and Jesus' revelation to John is that this sin-filled world must end for God to finally complete the creation He began in Genesis.

DID THE SAME PERSON WRITE JOHN'S GOSPEL, EPISTLES, AND REVELATION?

Tradition tells us that Jesus' apostle John was the author of about 20 percent of the New Testament. His works include the most religious and only nonsynoptic Gospel, three letters to early churches, and a record of his apocalyptic vision. That's three separate genres written over forty years between 70 CE and 110 CE.

Scholars have questioned whether or not one man could be responsible for all this writing. Revelation is the only book literally ascribed to a "John"; the others were written by John according to tradition. The Gospel only refers to its author in the third person as "the disciple whom Jesus loved," and the epistles give no indication of their author except that they are similar enough to the Gospel in style and vocabulary that most assume all were written by the same person. But was that person John, son of Zebedee, Jesus' apostle?

Modern scholarship contends that the Gospel and letters were written by the apostle, but that the Revelation was more likely written by a wandering prophet whose name happened to be John. It was a common name in the first century, as it is now, and the writing style is much less sophisticated than that of the Gospel and epistles.

Does it matter whether or not John the apostle wrote the Revelation? No. Whoever the author, that man was gifted with prophecy, had an inspired vision, and recorded the last book of Scripture. That act alone makes him not only a prophet but an apostle as well. He just might not have been one of the first twelve.

Unsanctioned Practices

The actual apocalyptic prophecies in Revelation and Daniel were not given so that we would ask how or when the end will come, as we tend to do, but *why*. Obscure, as-yet-unknowable imagery may distract us so that we forget that all prophecies in the Bible exist to bring us closer to God. He tells us what He tells us—and nothing more—because both the stated and unstated words are somehow a part of His plan to destroy sin, reconcile humanity to Himself, and live among us on an earth He creates.

But humanity has a long history of not being satisfied with what God has given to us. We may appreciate what He has done, but we want to take control of it. And figuring out the future for ourselves seems to be a great way to start.

Since we all didn't go poof on December 21, 2012, as the Mayan calendar seemed to predict, many more dates have been incorrectly suggested as the last day of the planet. There was September 23, 2017:

> Mr Meade, who wrote the book *Planet X—The 2017 Arrival*, claims the solar eclipse of August 21 was a sign before Nibiru appears in the sky to everyone from September 23, before passing and causing the apocalypse in October.
>
> He claims the September 23 date came from codes in the Bible and also a "date marker" shown by the pyramids of Giza in Egypt.
>
> Planet X, or Nibiru, is reportedly a huge planet with a vast orbit that conspiracy theorists claim will one day

pass so close to Earth that its gravitational pull could wreak havoc on our planet, triggering earthquakes and other catastrophic events.

Mr Meade said: "It is very strange indeed that both the Great Sign of Revelation 12 and the Great Pyramid of Giza both point us to one precise moment in time—September 20 to 23, 2017."[5]

And June 24, 2018:

Conspiracy theorist Mathieu Jean-Marc Joseph Rodrigue has highlighted a passage in the Book of Revelations [sic] as a sign that 2018 could be the Earth's last year. It reads: "He was given authority to act for 42 months."

Mr Joseph Rodrigue reckons the passage from Revelations [sic] when added to the crop harvest and price indicates a shocking truth...

To find the date of the apocalypse, he takes the 666 figure and adds it to his earlier calculations, with the 42 months from the bible. When all added together, he claims this indicates the world will end on June 24, 2018.

Despite his bold theory, Mr Joseph Rodrigue has not detailed how the world will come to destruction.[6]

More predictions will come and go because humans want to be all-knowing the way God is all-knowing. You probably aren't one of those people driving herself crazy trying to predict the future. You may not visit mediums or read the Bible for secret codes or try to calculate when an asteroid might obliterate the earth. But have you ever gone to the Bible looking for a specific answer to a specific question? Such as, *should I get married?* Or, *why did my friend die?* Maybe even, *should I buy this car right now?*

If God intended the Bible to be our Basic Instructions Before Leaving Earth, as the acrostic goes, then it is about as helpful as a poorly translated IKEA diagram. The Bible is not a "user's manual" for our lives but an intimate, mysterious, and complex picture of Him. To be able to discern how He is guiding our futures, we need a relationship with Him. We shouldn't go to our Bibles' indexes or Strong's Concordance and look up words such as *love* or *death* and expect to flip to each occurrence of the word and suddenly understand divine mysteries. God doesn't work that way, and neither does His Scripture. Quite frankly, it is rude to treat the Bible as we do dictionaries and encyclopedias.

Maybe reference-book divination isn't your thing, but you like to make deals with God. I've been guilty of this one many times. David and I spent seven years trying to have children. Almost every night I would lie in bed telling God that if He gave us a child, I would do *x*, *y*, or *z*. My most brilliant example of "biblical bargaining" was when I would pray Hannah's prayer and promise God I would raise my son as if he were a Nazirite: "O LORD of hosts, if You will indeed look on the affliction of Your maidservant and remember me, and not forget Your maidservant, but will give Your maidservant a male child, then I will give him to the LORD all the days of his life, and no razor shall come upon his head" (1 Samuel 1:11).

Even if God had spoken up at that moment and told me I would never carry a child to full term, I doubt it would have changed my behavior. Had He told me every detail about my future—when, where, why, and how—I still would have tried to take control because, like the Israelites worshipping Him from unsanctioned high places, I was looking for an easy way to get what I wanted. But God wanted me to come to His "temple" and worship Him, not my own desires. I needed to learn that I don't have faith in Him just so my life turns out as I want it to, but that faith turns my life to serve His purposes.

I've said it before, and I'll say it many more times: we must be content with saying "I don't know," because God doesn't intend for us to know everything right now. He has given us ways of discerning His will, mainly through Scripture and prayer, but those require patience.

Gone are the Old Testament days of drawing lots, visiting necromancers, and even dissecting animals for information about the future. Though most Christians overtly condemn all types of divination, from the ancient practices to medieval tarot cards and modern horoscope apps, too many of us flip through the Bible in times of confusion expecting Scripture to be a holy Magic 8-Ball or troubleshooting guide. Instead, we must practice consistent Bible study so that we are sensitive to God's Word and confident in our faith when questions arise.

Questions for Discussion and Reflection

1. Fortune-tellers, horoscopes, and mediums have been in this world almost as long as sin has because they feed off individuals' desires for divine knowledge of good and evil. Have you ever sought information about the future from God-disapproved sources? How did you respond to the illicit answers you received?

2. The Bible is full of examples of humans trying to influence God and get what they want instead of what He plans to give. In what ways have you tried to

bend God to your will? Did you ever feel you'd been successful?

3. God's Word tells us what He wants us to know and not always what we want Him to tell us; His omniscience is a big part of what makes Him God. How do you live with the uncertainties of life? Are you comfortable saying "I don't know" when God keeps His plans to Himself?

Chapter 8

TOO MANY COOKBOOKS IN THE CHRISTIAN KITCHEN

I n 2016 my in-laws got together on Thanksgiving Day as usual for the family feast. Everyone has their favorite dishes they like to bring to the table, but that year was different from previous years as our turkey specialist had moved with her husband and son to Colorado Springs. Everyone had a reason to say "not it!" to preparing the protein as we were dividing up the menu items among all the families, but my sister-in-law, Jess, volunteered. She would go on to prepare a thirty-pound turkey that year. Jess selected a Pioneer Woman recipe for the turkey, and it was by far the tastiest, juiciest turkey any of us had ever eaten. She is our family's new turkey specialist and will likely be so for the rest of her life.

What made Jess's turkey even more memorable was the fact that it was the first turkey she'd ever cooked. As most of us do when attempting new recipes, Jess followed every instruction to the letter. She brined it for twenty-four hours the day before. She rubbed it with herbs and olive oil inside and out. She stuffed it with oranges and had figured out exactly when the bird needed to go into the oven to be ready for the meal. She also asked that three of us bring along our meat thermometers; we had one stuck in a breast, thigh, and leg just in case Jess's instant-read failed and the button never popped. (Not that any of us were naive enough to trust a plastic factory-inserted button.)

A cookbook is necessary for every novice chef and every seasoned chef attempting something new. Until you have a recipe memorized and techniques mastered, you can't stray too far from the instructions. I learned my cooking techniques from my mother, but I owe most of my baking skills to recipes themselves. The more recipes I've read and practiced, the more I've learned.

I baked my first cheesecake when I was twelve years old. It was a special recipe my mother had gotten from a friend, and it became the foundation of my kitchen adventures. It taught me how to temper chocolate, execute the creaming method, and use a water bath. Those are skills I now use for lots of different dishes, whether or not the recipe suggests them.

I enjoy having the freedom to stray from the exact specifications on a recipe. David and I watched Alton Brown's *Good Eats* for years, and he taught us why foods react with each other and to different stimuli in the ways that they do. Why does the creaming method work? Why should eggs be room temperature before they are added? Why are there so many different types of flour—all purpose, self-rising, cake—in the wheat family alone? *Good Eats* inspired David to experiment with pancake recipes. He now makes the best traditional buttermilk pancakes in the world, but developing the new recipe meant breaking the rules of the recipes from which he started and trusting in the science of baking.

David's perfect pancakes are no more or less pancakes than the ones that come from the recipes he augmented. My cheesecakes are no less cheesecakey than the ones pictured in cookbooks just because I use a water bath while they bake. It is okay to stray from the rules of a recipe as long as the basics remain intact. This is good news for all my gluten-sensitive and lactose-free friends, as almond flour and coconut oil are the base ingredients of David's second-most-requested pancake recipe.

Denominationalism

If denominations are like pancakes—coming in all shapes, sizes, and flavors but never more than wet dough dropped onto a hot griddle—then the Bible is like the recipe we fight over.

When we study the words of our Bibles, we have a tendency to read between the lines. That's how you end up with so many Christians believing Mary Magdalene was a prostitute and Jesus was born in a barn. People with shared beliefs, whether they are right or wrong, find each other and form groups. And that's how you end up with nine thousand Protestant denominations,[1] each believing they better understand and better worship God than the other 8,999. We need to be wary of mistaking consensus for correctness.

In chapter 1 we talked about canonization and how different branches of the church read different books of the Bible. Protestants have the smallest Bible with sixty-six books, Catholics add the seven books of the Deuterocanon to their Old Testament, and Orthodox Christians read as many as thirteen more books than the Catholics do, depending on their region of the world. These branches of Christianity all started out wanting pancakes for breakfast, but they weren't even starting from the same recipe.

Did you catch the number of Protestant denominations? Nine thousand. Each denomination starts with the same Bible as their recipe for Christianity, but there are nine thousand cooks in that kitchen arguing over the ingredients and the methods. All the divisiveness comes from people following other people's beliefs and not Jesus Himself. This is not a new problem; following one leader of the Christian movement over another caused division from the moment Jesus resurrected. That is why Paul kept reminding his readers not to follow him or other disciples or apostles, but to follow Jesus only.

At the same time Paul was preaching, there was an Egyptian Jewish Christian named Apollos traveling throughout the region.

> This man had been instructed in the way of the Lord; and being fervent in spirit, he spoke and taught accurately the things of the Lord, though he knew only the baptism of John. So he began to speak boldly in the synagogue. When Aquila and Priscilla heard him, they took him aside and explained to him the way of God more accurately. And when he desired to cross to Achaia, the brethren wrote, exhorting the disciples to receive him; and when he arrived, he greatly helped those who had believed through grace; for he vigorously refuted the Jews publicly, showing from the Scriptures that Jesus is the Christ (Acts 18:25-28).

Apollos would go on to be an important Christian leader in the first century, even if he was not an apostle. He appears in the book of Acts and Paul's first letter to the Corinthians. Paul encourages the young Christians not to devote themselves to the teachings of any one person—no matter how righteous he may have been—but to focus on Jesus:

> Now I plead with you, brethren, by the name of our Lord Jesus Christ, that you all speak the same thing, and that there be no divisions among you, but that you be perfectly joined together in the same mind and in the same judgment. For it has been declared to me concerning you, my brethren, by those of Chloe's household,

that there are contentions among you. Now I say this, that each of you says, "I am of Paul," or "I am of Apollos," or "I am of Cephas [Peter]," or "I am of Christ." Is Christ divided? Was Paul crucified for you? Or were you baptized in the name of Paul?...

For Christ did not send me to baptize, but to preach the gospel, not with wisdom of words, lest the cross of Christ should be made of no effect (1 Corinthians 1:10-13,17).

Paul must be extremely disappointed in how Christians have ignored his advice for the last two thousand years. Jesus all the more so.

In most of the cases where a person's thoughts and writings have come to be revered almost as highly as Jesus', it is not necessarily that person's fault because God certainly gifts some people with the abilities to preach, teach, and discern Scripture (Ephesians 4:11). The fault lies at the feet of the followers who find it easier to understand and admire another human, instead of the unseen Christ. Doing so means valuing theology over faith, "-isms" over a unified church. Let's examine some examples from within the Protestant church.

Lutheranism

The first person to really get attention for saying, "Hey Christians! All this religion stuff is hindering and not helping our relationships with God," was Martin Luther. He was a Catholic monk and theology professor who, legend says, nailed a copy of the "Disputation of Martin Luther on the Power and Efficacy of Indulgences" (now commonly called the "Ninety-five Theses") onto the door of All Saints Church in Wittenberg, Germany, on October 31, 1517.

What probably started out as a private communication with the local bishop over Luther's concern that the Catholic Church was too money hungry became the pamphlet that launched Protestantism (with the help of that newfangled printing press). Instead of reforming the Catholic Church from inside, as he seemingly intended to do, a soon-excommunicated Martin Luther would launch a global Christian movement popularizing doctrines that contradicted sixteenth-century Catholicism and somewhat unify Protestant churches to this day.

The writings of Luther and those Reformers who would follow him agreed on five principles, which are today called the Five Solas:

1. *Sola Scriptura* ("by Scripture alone"): All Christian beliefs must come from the Bible. Any church traditions, creeds, and teachings must completely agree with Scripture.

2. *Sola Fide* ("by faith alone"): Reconciliation with God comes only from faith. It cannot be earned through works or purchased with tithes.

3. *Sola Gratia* ("by grace alone"): Reconciliation with God is a function of His grace. We cannot influence Him.

4. *Solus Christus* ("by Christ alone"): Reconciliation with God was only accomplished through Jesus' work on the cross. We can do nothing ourselves to earn it.

5. *Soli Deo Gloria* ("by the glory of God alone"): Everything a Christian says, does, or creates should glorify God. We should seek to accomplish His will and not our own.

Today's Lutheran church is the third-largest of the Protestant denominations. Although its modern practices have been influenced by almost five hundred years of tradition, its doctrines are the closest of any Protestant denomination to those of their namesake, Martin Luther.

Anglicanism

In 1534, a mere fourteen years after Luther was excommunicated from the Catholic Church, Henry VIII of England "excommunicated" the Catholic Church from England as he was declared Supreme Head of the Church of England by Parliament. Although the official reason for creating the Church of England was to formally distinguish the beliefs and practices of the island nation from its Catholic European enemies, King Henry's practical reason for forming the Anglican Church was to eliminate the pope's oversight of English policies and actions.

At that time Henry was married to Catherine of Aragon, a Spanish princess and devout Catholic with close ties to the pope, but he was in love with Anne Boleyn, a younger English woman who embraced the new Protestant ideas. When Henry asked the pope to annul his and Catherine's marriage based on questionable biblical arguments, the pope refused. So Henry joined the burgeoning Protestant movement, founded a new church, and made himself theologian-in-chief so he could marry, murder, and divorce women as he pleased.

The practices of the Church of England weren't dramatically different from those of the Catholic Church until Henry's son, Edward VI, ushered in the English Reformation. Henry's daughter, Elizabeth I, institutionalized the reforms by signing the Act of Uniformity in 1558, which she intended to bridge the differences between English Catholics and English Protestants. The differences between the two churches were outlined in the Thirty-Nine Articles, which were adopted by Parliament in 1571. Anglicans officially believed that:

- The English monarch is the head of the church, not the pope.

- Church services are to be conducted in the local language, not in Latin.
- Catholic traditions such as purgatory are incorrect.
- The Nicene, Athanasian, and Apostles' Creeds are truth because they are fully supported by Scripture.
- Clergy may marry and have families.

As the British Empire spread into other nations, so did the Anglican Church. It would go on to be influenced by the thoughts of John Calvin but would retain many Catholic doctrines and practices—such as the formal ordination of bishops, priests, and deacons—which other Protestant traditions rejected. In America, the Anglican movement developed into the Episcopal Church and was the forerunner of the Reformed denominations.

Calvinism

Born in France in 1509, John Calvin was well educated in the fields of philosophy, theology, and law. After converting from Catholicism to Lutheranism and publishing his famous *Institutes of the Christian Religion*, he was run out of France for his Protestant beliefs in 1536. Calvin would live out most of his life in Geneva, where he worked with the city elders to form a theocratic society based on his views of and writings about Scripture that infiltrated all aspects of every citizen's life. He died in 1564, but his work was the foundation of Puritanism and influenced theologians such as George Whitefield and Karl Barth.[2]

I was raised in a Calvinist congregation, but I didn't really learn about John Calvin until my junior-year high-school English class. In order to understand *The Scarlet Letter*, we had to know about Puritanism and John Calvin's five points of Christianity as represented by the acrostic TULIP:

- Total depravity of man: All of humanity was subject to Adam and Eve's first sin as described in Genesis 2–3. We are all in need of salvation but can only choose evil.

- Unconditional election: Even before God created us, He chose which humans will know Him and which will not, which will be saved and which will be damned. This is commonly called "election" or "predestination" in theological circles.

- Limited atonement: Jesus died only to save those whom God had chosen to be saved before creation.

- Irresistible grace: Those whom God has chosen for salvation cannot resist the call of the Holy Spirit. They literally cannot say no to salvation.

- Perseverance of the saints: Anyone chosen by God for salvation remains saved; he or she cannot stray from God and will be in heaven after death.

These five points are followed by churches with words such as "Presbyterian" or "Reformed" in their names. About 30 percent of Southern Baptists consider themselves Calvinists as well.

Arminianism

Jacob Arminius was a toddler in Holland when John Calvin died. He spent his early twenties questioning the five points of Calvinism at the Geneva Academy, which Calvin had founded, but he left without achieving a degree. Back home in Holland, while he was working as a minister, Arminius settled his mind that Jesus died for everyone, grace can be rejected, and salvation can be lost. He died in 1609, but his writings persisted and influenced theologians such as John and Charles Wesley.[3]

It is oversimplifying the writings of any theologian to boil them down to five points, but that is exactly what Arminius's followers did the year after he died to refute the Calvinism that was so popular in Holland at the time:

- Article I (Conditional election): God has chosen all of humanity to receive salvation through His grace, but we must choose to accept that grace. The exercise of choice is commonly called "free will" in theological circles.

- Article II (Unlimited atonement): Jesus died to save all who choose to accept His atonement for their sins.

- Article III (Deprivation): All of humanity was affected by Adam and Eve's first sin as described in Genesis 2–3. We are all in need of salvation, but we can be transformed by God's grace, which reignites free will.

- Article IV (Resistible grace): God's offer of salvation is free to all who choose not to resist the call of the Holy Spirit. They literally can say no to salvation.

- Article V (Assurance and security): All who choose God's salvation have it as long as they remain faithful to God and never reject Him.

Congregations that call themselves Wesleyan, Methodist, Pentecostal, or Nazarene traditionally accept these doctrines.

Evangelicalism

Not all "-isms" carry the names of their founders. There was no one named "Anglican"—the word is essentially a synonym for *English*—just as there was no one named "Evangelical" who founded the amorphous Evangelical Christian movement.

Someone who doesn't know very much about Protestant

denominations but watches the evening news would be justified in thinking *evangelicalism* is nothing more than a demographic. Political poll numbers are often broken down by gender, age, race, and "evangelicals." One would expect that last category to be "religion," but no, it's usually "evangelicals." It is anyone's guess as to whom exactly the pollsters lump into that group.

Evangelicalism has been around since the late eighteenth century. Pastors such as John Wesley in England and Jonathan Edwards in America used "fire and brimstone" messages to remind Christians of death's hellish horrors awaiting anyone who did not believe in Jesus' sacrifice and resurrection. In the nineteenth century, missionary work and social activism became hallmarks of evangelicalism, leading to the abolition of slavery and the founding of organizations such as the Salvation Army. By the twentieth century, the movement refocused on theology and the inerrancy of Scripture. Tent and street revivals became popular, and the world met the great Billy Graham.

Evangelicalism was and is pan-Christian. Entire denominations such as the Methodists and Pentecostals developed because of it, and to this day there are at least some Protestants from all mainline denominations who consider themselves evangelical. But a movement that may have had the chance of unifying diverse, disagreeing Christians has been so badly stereotyped, caricatured, and denigrated by the world that many Christians who are evangelical in their beliefs and actions shy away from the label today.

Pastor Perfect-isms

All congregations, regardless of their denomination, run the risk of venerating their local pastor or a popular Christian televangelist or author. That is precisely what Paul was warning the early Christians against. No divisive "-isms" had really developed yet, but it seems based on 1 Corinthians that a lot of first-century people were picking their favorite apostle or disciple to follow.

Like Paul and Luther and Calvin and Arminius, many of today's Christian leaders and thinkers have large followings because they espouse sound theology. Congregations and readers are attracted to their work because the Holy Spirit is working through them. Some of these Christian theologians actively preach against the borderline hero worship that has made them famous, as Paul did. Sadly, others are selfishly monetizing their positions as leaders by telling congregants what they want to hear in order to grow their numbers and raise donations. (Obviously that second group I'm describing contains those prosperity theologians and their proof-texting that we discussed in chapter 3.)

An embarrassing example of this came to light in 2018 as some pastors were exposed for asking their followers to donate money for private jets. One pastor, Jesse Duplantis of Louisiana, went so far as to claim that "if the Lord Jesus Christ was physically on the Earth today, he wouldn't be riding a donkey. He'd be in an airplane flying all over the world."[4] Sadly, this preacher who claims to have almost three million followers all over the world is not acquainted with Jesus' actual instructions to His apostles: "Take nothing for the journey, neither staffs nor bag nor bread nor money; and do not have two tunics apiece. Whatever house you enter, stay there, and from there depart. And whoever will not receive you, when you go out of that city, shake off the very dust from your feet as a testimony against them" (Luke 9:3-5).

No matter which theologian is your favorite—even if it is your own church's pastor—realize that quoting his or her words is not the same as quoting the inspired Word of God. So before hanging your faith on the Sunday-morning teachings or bestselling books of any human, ask yourself if you would draw the same conclusions about faith and works, election or prosperity, jets or donkeys, or anything else he or she says by simply reading Scripture. If you can't follow the logic, then you shouldn't blindly follow that preacher. Save your faith for what God actually said in Scripture, and not what any human says about Him.

Legalism

Paul was concerned about people claiming individuals as their leaders and not Jesus alone, and what followed showed that his concern was justified. Jesus followers split from the Jews, then divided into Orthodox and Catholics and Protestants, then subdivided into tens of thousands of denominations across the entire (not just Protestant) Christian spectrum.[5]

Too often Christians tie themselves in knots trying to justify their own beliefs that may be scriptural but more often are based on tradition or opinion. We've already addressed several such issues in this book, including creation (chapter 2), Bible translation (chapter 3), and prophecy (chapter 7). Those are foundational issues that make us ask who are we as humans, how we should read God's Word, and how He speaks to us. But most of what Christians fight over are behaviors that may or may not be sins.

When we don't like the ways that other people act, it is easy to label their actions as sinful whether they are or not. A popular example of this is some denominations' prohibition against drinking alcohol. The logic goes something like this: Drinking might lead to drunkenness, and drunkenness is a sin. Even if drinking doesn't make you drunk, others may see you drink, assume it is okay, and become drunk themselves. Their sins would then be your fault. This idea comes from a proof-texting of Romans 14:21: "It is good neither to eat meat nor drink wine nor do anything by which your brother stumbles or is offended or is made weak." Even by itself, verse 21 does not call potentially contagious behavior sinful; Paul just says it is not "good." Let's look at the verse in its context:

> In light of this, we must resolve never to judge others and never to place an obstacle or impediment in their paths that could cause them to trip and fall. Personally I have been completely convinced that in Jesus, our Lord, no object in and of itself is unclean; but if my fellow believers are convinced that something is unclean, then it is unclean to them. If the food you eat harms your brother, then you have failed to love him. Do not let what you eat tear down your brother; after all, the Anointed laid down His life for him. Do not allow people to slander something you find to be good because the kingdom of God is not about eating and drinking. *When God reigns, the order of the day is* redeeming justice, true peace, and joy made possible by the Holy Spirit. You see, those who serve the Anointed in this way will be welcomed into the whole acceptance of God and valued by all men. Join us, and pursue a life that creates peace and builds up our brothers and sisters.
>
> Do not sacrifice God's work for the sake of certain foods. *It is true that* all things are clean, but it's wrong to eat if you know that eating something will cause offense. It is right for you to abstain from certain meats and wine (or anything else for that matter) if it prevents your brother from falling *in his faith.* Hold on to what you believe *about these issues,* but keep them between you and God. A happy man does not judge himself by the lifestyle he endorses. But a man who decides for himself what to eat is condemned because he is not living by his faith. Any action not consistent with faith is sin (Romans 14:13-23 THE VOICE).

Paul isn't talking about drinking at all; he is telling us how to love one another and unify all people within the church. We Christians should be willing to surrender our freedoms if doing so will build up those around us. Love is more important than personal liberty.

While I would never say that churches should promote the consumption of alcohol—it can be both addictive and bad for your health—they are wrong to cite Scripture as the reason for everyone abstaining. The Bible does call drunkenness foolish and warn against it, but it is never labeled as *sin*. The most commonly cited verse used to convince people not to drink (or do a lot of other dangerous things) is 1 Corinthians 6:9-10: "Do you not know that the unrighteous will not inherit the kingdom of God? Do not be deceived. Neither fornicators, nor idolaters, nor adulterers, nor homosexuals, nor sodomites, nor thieves, nor covetous, nor drunkards, nor revilers, nor extortioners will inherit the kingdom of God." If you read Paul's words as they are copied here, to the exclusion of the rest of the letter or even just the rest of chapter 6, then it appears that drunkenness will keep us all out of heaven.

UNITY OF SCRIPTURE

Scripture cannot contradict itself because God is righteous. We may not always understand how different parts of Scripture fit together or why manuscripts disagree with each other on the little things, but that's okay because we don't fully understand God either.

The Bible states that many people drank wine, including Noah (Genesis 9:20-21), Abraham (Genesis 14:18-20), and Isaac (Genesis 27:25). It also tells us that they have places in heaven:

These all died in faith, not having received the promises,

but having seen them afar off were assured of them, embraced them and confessed that they were strangers and pilgrims on the earth. For those who say such things declare plainly that they seek a homeland. And truly if they had called to mind that country from which they had come out, they would have had opportunity to return. But now they desire a better, that is, a heavenly country. Therefore God is not ashamed to be called their God, **for He has prepared a city for them** (Hebrews 11:13-16, emphasis added).

You probably also know that Jesus made wine for a wedding in Cana, and it was "good wine" (John 2:1-12), not plain grape juice that would not have intoxicated the guests. I once had a Sunday school teacher insist that this and all Bible wine was nonalcoholic. That didn't make much sense to me even as a child. Thanks to a poorly sealed bottle of Welch's that my grandmother had bought accidentally one Christmas, I had learned that refrigeration was the only thing to stop juice from fermenting if the air hadn't been vacuumed out of the container. In the ancient Near East, the closest thing they had to a refrigerator was a hole in the ground, and there was no tool to seal the porous pottery jars or wineskins that stored the juices.

If Paul or any other New Testament writer had meant to prohibit all Christians from drinking, then he would have been in disagreement with the rest of Scripture, and his words would not be part of the Christian canons.

But read that verse within its context:

You yourselves do wrong and cheat, and you do these

things to your brethren! Do you not know that the unrighteous will not inherit the kingdom of God? Do not be deceived. Neither fornicators, nor idolaters, nor adulterers, nor homosexuals, nor sodomites, nor thieves, nor covetous, nor drunkards, nor revilers, nor extortioners will inherit the kingdom of God. And such were some of you. But you were washed, but you were sanctified, but you were justified in the name of the Lord Jesus and by the Spirit of our God.

All things are lawful for me, but all things are not helpful. All things are lawful for me, but I will not be brought under the power of any. Foods for the stomach and the stomach for foods, but God will destroy both it and them. Now the body is not for sexual immorality but for the Lord, and the Lord for the body. And God both raised up the Lord and will also raise us up by His power (1 Corinthians 6:8-14).

Paul tells some of his readers—who are Christians—that they are drunkards. How can they be Christians *and* be drunkards? Because they were "washed," "sanctified," and "justified in the name of the Lord Jesus and by the Spirit of our God." That's a rather important part of Paul's writing that pretty much destroys all legalistic judgments of personal behavior.

However, he goes on to say "all things are lawful," but "all things are not helpful." Drinking alcohol will not unwash, unsanctify, or unjustify us, but it is not necessarily good for us either. It can cause us to act like fools (Proverbs 20:1), commit other actual sins (Genesis 19:30-38), and be generally poor representatives of God and His kingdom.

Dangerous behavior may not keep us from being saved, but because it usually reflects badly on the church family and often has negative physical and spiritual side effects, humans have decided to twist Scripture into outlawing what God has allowed. This is *legalism*, which is dependence on subjective morality instead of faith in God's grace. Legalism treats the actions that Paul calls "unhelpful" as if they are "unlawful."

Paul gives a rather lengthy list of unhelpful actions in 1 Corinthians, but a lot of the church has added even to that. The *Footloose* town certainly isn't the only place that frowns on dancing, and I've seen a church (in Denver, of all places) turn away someone with exposed tattoos. How many houses of worship have two different Sunday services listed on their signs—one traditional and one contemporary—because half the body thinks nonhymnal music does not honor God while the other half thinks nonhymnal music is the only way to praise Him? How one chooses to worship isn't even an issue of "unhelpful" behavior; it's just personal preference. There is no right or wrong.

We all find ourselves unfairly judged from time to time. In my adult life I have encountered legalism twice, neither of which would have been a problem if I were not a woman. The first time was back in 2008. David and I were attending a church that had a lot of very traditional Christians in the congregation. Although some women covered their heads in service, I had somehow missed just how literally one family took the words, "Let your women keep silent in the churches, for they are not permitted to speak; but they are to be submissive, as the law also says. And if they want to learn something, let them ask their own husbands at home; for it is shameful for women to speak in church" (1 Corinthians 14:34-35). One Sunday I stood in the pulpit at the end of service to make an announcement about a church dinner I had been asked to coordinate. The family complained to some elders loudly enough for me to hear about it the next week, and then they left the church for a few years.

I think most Christians would agree that the family's reaction was extreme. I was not preaching or praying; I was inviting everyone to a dinner the church itself had asked me to organize and announce.

That dinner went really well, and as the church leadership got to know David and me better, they started trusting us with more responsibilities within the church. By 2009 David and I were leading a small group of men and women in our home every other Friday. Because I was the one with a theology degree, I tended to guide discussion and answer questions about Scripture. I didn't consider that "ministry" (in hindsight, of course it was), so I was always surprised when someone would hear about our little group and complain to the elders about a woman teaching. My husband and the other husbands in the room were learning from me, and not the other way around (1 Corinthians 14:35).

To their credit, the elders of this sometimes-head-covering church always supported me, even if they didn't know what to do with me. During those seven years, I know of not one but two families who left the church because of me, but never was I censured or reprimanded—only loved and encouraged by the leaders of a church that I, too, loved so much. Those were years of dynamic spiritual growth for everyone in our small group, David and me especially. The way I see it, the legalism of those families who had a problem with my making an announcement or knowing Hebrew only made them miserable.

THE IMPORTANCE OF TRADITION

Tradition is the living faith of the dead; traditionalism is the dead faith of the living. Tradition lives in conversation with the past, while remembering where we are and when we are and that it is we who have to decide.

> Traditionalism supposes that nothing should ever be
> done for the first time, so all that is needed to solve any
> problem is to arrive at the supposedly unanimous testi-
> mony of this homogenized tradition.[6]

Tradition allows us to know why we believe or behave in the ways that we do, but it shouldn't dictate the future. Just because something "is that way" doesn't mean it should always be that way. This is especially true in the church. The popular songs we sing, books we read, and speakers we listen to today will be at best stale and at worst fallen from grace tomorrow. Just imagine if the Singing Nun was arranging our worship services, Hal Lindsey was teaching our Revelation classes, and Jim Bakker and Jimmy Swaggart were still our favorite televangelists (or that we paid attention to televangelists at all).

Very little that is popular stands the test of time and remains relevant to all communities in perpetuity. Scripture is one such rare gem, as is Christian liturgy. All branches of Christianity practice at least two liturgical rites: the Lord's Supper (also known as Communion and the Eucharist) and baptism. These traditions, though expressed differently among the denominations, began with first-century followers of Jesus and are still practiced regularly by the church.

Some Protestant denominations, including Lutheran, Anglican, and Methodist, use verbal liturgies in their services that echo the words that have been spoken by Christians with the same beliefs for generations. Many more regularly recite the Lord's Prayer; the foundational Nicene, Athanasian, and Apostles' Creeds; and sing songs such as the doxology that remind the church of exactly what Christianity is and why they worship God. These ancient practices connect the worshipper not only to God but to the millions of Christians who have ever believed the same words anywhere in the world at any time since Jesus taught us to pray, "Our Father who art in heaven, hallowed be Your Name..."

Maybe it comes from being an archaeologist and having an innate love of all things antiquated, but I always try to understand the past and respect it. Within a church family, that means appreciating the people who have come before me, learning why they chose to do things in the ways they did, and respecting them for how they've served. If the seniors in your church love singing with a pipe organ and from physical hymnals, then try to enjoy it with them. Our elders have a lot to teach us about both wrong and right, and the better we honor them, the more we can learn from them.

So should women speak or teach in the church? Is my Hebrew degree somehow "unhelpful" even if it is not sinful? In their quests to give women equality in the church, a lot of theologians will declare that Paul was a misogynist and then ignore everything he wrote about women. I'm not going to do that because I believe the Bible is the inspired Word of God—even when what it says is hard for me to hear. We can't use the Bible to justify our own questionable behaviors, just as we shouldn't use it to tell other people their actions will send them to hell. That is for the Holy Spirit to do. But I also won't read the "women should be silent" verses (1 Corinthians 14:34-36 and 1 Timothy 2:9-15) in isolation from their contexts. I hope by now I've shown that is a poor way to interact with Scripture.

As we find with a lot of today's social issues, there is no definitive answer to how much responsibility women should have in churches. When determining women's roles in the church, we must consider what Paul wrote but also how women are portrayed in general throughout the New Testament. Doing that, we end up with seeming contradictions that no theologian has ever adequately explained.

Paul writes very clearly that the women in the churches of Corinth and Ephesus in the first century needed to be quiet. What you read in your English translations is indeed a good reflection of what is found in the Greek. But we can't take just those verses—by themselves—as commands apart from biblical context, because it is obvious that women such as Priscilla were leaders and teachers of men and women. Priscilla schooled Apollos, one of the great Christian teachers of the first century, when she and her husband "took him aside and explained to him the way of God more accurately" (Acts 18:26). Scripture doesn't say that her husband took Apollos aside while Priscilla stood there quietly trying to learn something herself. She did half of the explaining!

To reconcile why Paul appreciated Priscilla's Christian leadership enough to greet her by name in three of his letters (Romans 16:3, 1 Corinthians 16:19, and 2 Timothy 4:19) but seemingly told all other women to keep their mouths closed, many scholars turn to historical criticism. Paul is writing to the churches in Corinth and Ephesus because they were having trouble keeping order during their meetings. The reasons seem to differ: Corinth had a bunch of tongue-speakers and prophets who liked to hear themselves talk, and Ephesus had been infiltrated by false teachers. It may be that Paul was telling only those women in their specific circumstances to be silent as part of the churches' efforts to solve problems of chaos, gossip, and false teaching. But maybe he wasn't because those same issues affect every church on earth today. We simply cannot be certain.

Where there is uncertainty in the meaning of Scripture, we tend to form our own opinions and then force our answers—be they right or wrong—on everyone around us. When those opinions govern behavior, that's legalism.

Holy Spirit-ualism

Legalism is sweating the small stuff. It inflates the judge's pride, damns those who practice what may be "lawful" but "not helpful," and leaves no room for grace. To return to my cookbook metaphor of the Bible as a recipe, *legalism* means there can be no water-bath-baked cheesecakes or gluten-free, almond-flour pancakes. It elevates a human's personal opinion of what the text means over the grace of God and the influence of the Holy Spirit that refine the Bible's recipe for the achievement of God's will.

When it comes to God and baking, the basics are what matter most. As Paul wrote,

> Christ did not send me to baptize, but to preach the gospel, not with wisdom of words, lest the cross of Christ should be made of no effect. For the message of the cross is foolishness to those who are perishing, but to us who are being saved it is the power of God. For it is written:
>
> > "I will destroy the wisdom of the wise,
> > And bring to nothing the understanding of
> > the prudent."
>
> Where is the wise? Where is the scribe? Where is the disputer of this age? Has not God made foolish the wisdom of this world? For since, in the wisdom of God, the world through [its own] wisdom did not know God, it pleased God through the foolishness of the message preached to save those who believe (1 Corinthians 1:17-21, antecedent added).

Anything we humans concoct and push on others is pure fool-
ishness. God says so through Paul.

God, in His wisdom, sent Jesus to die so our sins were reconciled
like a red-summed checkbook balanced by a big family inheritance.
We did nothing to earn that "money"; grace saves us all as long as
we accept it. Christians should agree that Jesus' sacrifice is the only
thing that saves humanity, not how well we all behave or, thankfully,
how often we agree with one another. We should have less pride in
our opinions and more pride in Jesus' work for all of us.

When we stop relying on our own flawed interpretations of challenging Scriptures and (more importantly) stop judging others by
our personal and mundane interpretations, then we are forced to say
"I don't know" and trust that God is in control of His creation. We
must let go of our sinful pride-fueled needs to be gods ourselves and
let the Holy Spirit do the work of saving those around us. Scripture
does not charge us with saving one another; we are only asked to
accept and enjoy God's grace. Once we have it, the Holy Spirit may
become irresistible (as Calvin insisted) and then use our lives to further God's work of reconciling all of humanity to Himself. But that
can happen only if we get ourselves—that is, our pride in our own
questionable correctness—out of His way.

Jesus called us to love God and love each other (Luke 10:27).
God tells us to believe that Jesus' sacrifice has saved all who have
and will ever trust in it (John 3:16). That is Christianity. So when
we Christians—brothers and sisters who are all children of God—
disagree on laws or behaviors, let us pray that the Holy Spirit
makes the truth clear to whoever needs His correction and direc-
tion instead of chastising them ourselves. It is the Holy Spirit's job
to discipline individual Christians; we are only told to love each
other.

Most of the dissention between Christian denominations is due to churchgoers' stubborn devotions to ideologies, be they Catholic, Orthodox, Lutheran, Calvinist, Arminian, or any other branch of Christianity. Parishioners are often taught more about their churches' doctrines and leaders than about the Bible, and they may find it easier to follow the logic of long-dead theologians than to accept that God's Word is mysterious. Such devotion to other people's ideologies breeds Christians who know what they believe, but not necessarily why they believe it—Christians who are likely to become legalists themselves.

Salvation is not based on the words of dead humans, even if those words come from great Christians such as Martin Luther and Billy Graham. It is not governed by the behavioral preferences of denominations or legalists. Salvation results from Jesus' death and resurrection as Scripture alone can attest. All other beliefs and behaviors should be dictated by Scripture and the Holy Spirit and only guided by biblical theologians, Sunday school teachers, and gifted preachers.

In his letters, Paul frequently told Christians from all backgrounds to stop following men and start following Jesus. The church should be unified. This was Jesus' desire, too, and He prayed for it the night before His crucifixion:

> I do not pray for [the apostles] alone, but also for those who will believe in Me through their word; that they all may be one, as You, Father, are in Me, and I in You; that they also may be one in Us, that the world may believe that You sent Me. And the glory which You gave Me I have given them, that they may be one just as We are one: I in them, and You in Me; that they may be made perfect in one, and that the world may know that You

have sent Me, and have loved them as You have loved Me (John 17:20-23).

Jesus knew it would be impossible for Christians to accomplish godly unity on our own, so He asked God to help us. If ever the world saw large, diverse groups setting aside their petty differences to unite as Jesus and God unite within the Trinity, Jesus says the world would take notice of such a miracle. Christian unity has the potential to introduce the world to God, tell them about His Son, Jesus, and what He did, and show them that God loves them as He does His own Son. This is an opportunity for all Christians regardless of their denominations, not in spite of them.

Questions for Discussion and Reflection

1. The word *evangelicalism* has developed a negative connotation as media commentators and pollsters have conflated it with *legalism*, causing many actual evangelical Christians to shy away from the label. Are you an evangelical in the true historical sense, someone willing to cross denominational lines to accomplish missionary work and social activism?

2. When opinions are treated as truth, they can lead to legalism. Which of your personal opinions do you use to judge and chastise Christians who hold different opinions? How well do your attitudes reflect Jesus?

3. Tradition is useful when it connects us to and helps us understand the past, but what is tradition's place in the church? Should it be respected as law or rejected as stale? Might the church find a middle ground?

Chapter 9

THE GOD CONTEXT

I've avoided using one really big word in the previous eight chapters: *hermeneutics*. It just sounds so cold and clinical, as if this book should be hermetically sealed for your protection. No one ever wants to read sixty thousand words about hermeneutics, but if you've made it this far, then you just did. Whoops!

I tried to ease you into it with a lot of entertaining (to me) background information. Now you know how that leather-bound, gold-edged, ribbon-marked book on your shelf evolved from ancient oral tradition. You know what the Bible is and what it is not, how to read it and how not to read it. And maybe most importantly, you know how it is used and misused today. All of that is biblical hermeneutics.

Hermeneutics is the "art of understanding." Yes, *art*. The word may sound as if it dropped out of the medical textbook *Gray's Anatomy*, but there really is no hard science involved in understanding the Bible. Even biblical archaeology, which is the most science-y part of hermeneutics, is all about impression and interpretation.

In December 2017, as I was writing this book, my graduate advisor died. The very day I finished the manuscript, I received my bimonthly copy of *Biblical Archaeology Review* in the mail and read an article honoring his great work.[1] Larry Stager discovered the "golden calf" we discussed in chapter 4, and it was he who figured out the common layout of Israelite houses. He took me on my first trip to Israel and taught me a lot of the archaeological details you read in this book. He also showed me just how subjective archaeology can be.

I believe he was the first person who said to me about biblical archaeology, "If you go looking for it, then you will find it." That is not a good thing. Everything we picked, dug, brushed, and sifted out of the dirt was subject to interpretation. So if we had happened to find thirty bodies in a mass grave (we were in the formerly Philistine city of Ashkelon, after all), then we could have subconsciously figured out a way to link the discovery with Judges 14:19 ("[Samson] went down to Ashkelon and killed thirty of their men, took their apparel, and gave the changes of clothing to those who had explained the riddle") and "prove" Samson was there. That definitely is not a scientific method; and for the record, no such stilted logic was employed when I was at Ashkelon. But, as Professor Stager warned me, finding just what it is you are looking for is always a risk.

The study of the Bible itself can be the same way. If we read it expecting to see God as loving, then we will. If we think He is angry, then we will find that too. Without sound hermeneutics, Scripture can say just about anything we want it to say. That is why it is so important to read the Bible without preconceived notions, searching only for God's character as He presents it to us in Scripture.

God of His Own Stories

Several years ago, a friend of mine was preparing a sermon. He had been asked to speak to the congregation about the topic, "God of the Old Testament and God of the New Testament," and he was having trouble reconciling the two. He had done a lot of reading and research, and he had concluded that the Bible presents two totally different Gods.

The God in the Old Testament, my friend said, is an angry, fire-and-brimstone God. After the Exodus, as the Israelites are wandering the desert and receiving His 613 laws, God told them what to do when they (or their children) would eventually encounter foreign armies in their coming quest to conquer Canaan. He commanded them to murder entire nations of men, women, children, and animals:

> But of the cities of these peoples which the Lord your God gives you as an inheritance, you shall let nothing that breathes remain alive, but you shall utterly destroy them: the Hittite and the Amorite and the Canaanite and the Perizzite and the Hivite and the Jebusite, just as the Lord your God has commanded you, lest they teach you to do according to all their abominations which they have done for their gods, and you sin against the Lord your God (Deuteronomy 20:16-18).

After Israel was established as a nation, King David brought the ark of the covenant into Jerusalem with great fanfare. But when the cart carrying the ark tipped, God killed the man trying to save His ark from a damaging fall:

> Uzzah put out his hand to the ark of God and took hold of it, for the oxen stumbled. Then the anger of the Lord was aroused against Uzzah, and God struck him there for his error; and he died there by the ark of God. And David became angry because of the Lord's outbreak against Uzzah; and he called the name of the place Perez Uzzah to this day (2 Samuel 6:6-8).

These are just two of so many examples where God seems to be unjustly vengeful. Each story makes us ask, *How could God let this happen?*

My friend continued to tell me that the God of the New Testament, as he read it, was a loving and graceful God. He chose to return to His creation, in the Person of Jesus the Son, so He could save not just His Old Testament family but everyone in the world who would follow Him. While Jesus was on earth, He fed people and healed people, and then He sacrificed Himself. God—not God's enemies—was the one dying the painful death. He chose a most difficult way to reconcile humanity to Himself, and He did it out of love for all of us.

I understand why my friend said there seem to be two different Gods in the Bible; the Old Testament appears law-oriented while the New Testament reads as love-oriented. I've heard other people say, along the same lines, "I like what Jesus said and did, but I can't follow a God who ignores all the pain and suffering in this world." But as Christians, we cannot choose between God the Father and Jesus the Son. They are both God, along with the Holy Spirit. There is no separating the parts of the Trinity because all three Persons have always been and will always be One. The Eternal One—Yahweh.

WHERE'S THE TRINITY?

The word *trinity* does not appear anywhere in the Bible's text. It may be found in the footnotes or essays of study Bibles, but no Greek or Hebrew manuscripts contain it. Yet it is a fundamental part of Christian belief.

Early in the second century CE, the church leaders such as Ignatius and Justin Martyr began developing the concept. They needed to explain how Christians could worship one

God and simultaneously a Father, Son, and Holy Spirit. In the fourth century, after literally hundreds of years of squabbling over the details, the Council of Nicea decided that God the Father, God the Son, and God the Holy Spirit are co-equal and co-eternal. They are, as the hymn goes, "God in three Persons, blessed Trinity."[2] It is the earthly explanation of how there can be one God who exists in three incarnations. I find the doctrine impossible to fully understand, so it is one of those mysteries I choose to have faith in and hope to understand in heaven.

Similarly, all of the Bible is God's Word. All of the individual books and stories and laws and poems and epistles were written and compiled and copied by perhaps hundreds of people along the Bible's way to canonization. Those bits and pieces, jots and tittles fit together to form a well-rounded religious text that reveals our complex God. Each testament, each story, each song, and each letter reveal in one anthology a different aspect of the one eternal God.

We love learning about God being slow to anger and abounding in love. But as my friend discovered, some of those Old Testament stories reveal a God who is both righteously just and justifiably wrathful. Few of us are ever ready to read about the drowning of all but Noah's family in the Flood (Genesis 7:21-23) or the sacrifice of Jephthah's daughter (Judges 11:34-40), but even the hard-to-read stories are important. They remind us that God is righteous.

When we read the word *righteous*, we tend to give it a connotation of *fair*. But God isn't fair like Lady Justice, blindfolded and holding scales. He doesn't judge and sentence as a jury of our twelve American peers would. He is God, so He is right. There is no arguing with that reality. We won't always understand the whys and hows of what God does, but we aren't meant to do so. That's why we can say, "I don't know," without compromising our faith in His righteousness.

God of the Ignorant

When I was in middle school, I spent the night with my then-soon-to-be best friend Sara for the first time. She was in her bathroom with the light off, staring blankly into the mirror and brushing her teeth before we went to sleep, and I asked her if she wanted me to switch on the light. "I stay in the dark most of the time," she replied. It was a slip of the tongue that I have teased her about for the last twenty-five years.

Sara is one of the brightest people I know, in that she's both smart and a "light of the world" (Matthew 5:14-16). She dedicated her life to ministry in high school. None of her friends were surprised when she did because she's always had a kind spirit, and she certainly has kept her vow. Sara, her husband, and her two daughters inspire me with the ways they all serve God in almost every facet of their lives—at their jobs and schools, in their church, and in their home as a foster family. She is a woman of grace and faith who appears to be devoid of pride.

I say "appears to be" not because I think she's trying to fool anyone, but because I know that no matter how close she is to God, she is human. She was affected by the Fall just as I was and you were and every other human on this planet was. That Fall—when Eve and Adam ate from the tree of knowledge and let sin enter this world—was precipitated by pride. The first humans were living in a perfect garden with God, but it wasn't enough. They wanted to be gods. They wanted to know everything as He knows everything. That is what we all want deep down inside ourselves. Or maybe not so deep down, in some cases.

Until Jesus comes back, we all will "stay in the dark most of the time." Sara wasn't quoting the apostle Paul—"for now we see through a glass, darkly; but then face to face" (1 Corinthians 13:12 KJV)—but she could have been. Paul wrote 1 Corinthians 13 not so people would quote it at their weddings as the (cue Barry White's baritone) "luv chapter," but to remind the men and women of the church in Corinth that God gifted us all differently and reveals Himself to us differently so that we will work together as one church to accomplish His one will.

Paul's 1 Corinthians 13 has been used out of context so often that it has practically lost its meaning when read in a modern translation. This is one of the few parts of the Bible I truly prefer in the King James Version because "charity" is a better translation for today's readers than "love" is. When we read *love*, we automatically think of romantic love, and that is not the subject of this chapter. So score this one for the seventeenth century:

> Though I speak with the tongues of men and of angels, and have not charity, I am become as sounding brass, or a tinkling cymbal.

> And though I have the gift of prophecy, and understand all mysteries, and all knowledge; and though I have all faith, so that I could remove mountains, and have not charity, I am nothing.

> And though I bestow all my goods to feed the poor, and though I give my body to be burned, and have not charity, it profiteth me nothing.

> Charity suffereth long, and is kind; charity envieth not; charity vaunteth not itself, is not puffed up,

> Doth not behave itself unseemly, seeketh not her own, is not easily provoked, thinketh no evil;

Rejoiceth not in iniquity, but rejoiceth in the truth;

Beareth all things, believeth all things, hopeth all things, endureth all things.

Charity never faileth: but whether there be prophecies, they shall fail; whether there be tongues, they shall cease; whether there be knowledge, it shall vanish away.

For we know in part, and we prophesy in part.

But **when that which is perfect is come**, then that which is in part shall be done away.

When I was a child, I spake as a child, I understood as a child, I thought as a child: but when I became a man, I put away childish things.

For now we see through a glass, darkly; but then face to face: now I know in part; but **then shall I know even as also I am known**.

And now abideth faith, hope, charity, these three; but the greatest of these is charity (emphasis added).

When our beliefs are challenged by each other, by the church, or by the world, we can boldly say, "I don't know!" There is no shame in that answer because God does not intend for us to know everything right now. We will all be just a little—or maybe a lot—ignorant until the Second Coming.

It is better to say, "I don't know," than to be a false teacher who leads others away from God. Remember that James says "teachers will be held to a higher standard" (James 3:1 THE VOICE): teachers must know how to study the Bible for what God says and not just recite to students what they have been taught. Teachers should employ hermeneutics.

But just because ignorance is our current state doesn't mean we should settle into it. We should always be striving to know God better through reading, prayer, and action.

God of the Underdogs

There is no reason to fear the words "I don't know" or think we are incapable of serving God and humanity while we are on earth. God neither expects nor intends for us to understand everything about Him or His creation. Perfect knowledge is not necessary for God to use us, thank goodness; flexibility and dedication may make it easier for us to follow His lead, but God can and will use the stubborn and disobedient to accomplish His will (just ask Jonah!).

God has a habit of choosing underdogs and gifting the unexceptional to do the work of His kingdom. In the ancient Near East, customs dictated the oldest sons inherited their fathers' fortunes and blessings, but not in God's family. He chose Isaac over Ishmael, Jacob over Esau, Judah over Reuben, David over all his older brothers, Solomon over Adonijah...and the list goes on. Moses was "slow of speech and slow of tongue" (Exodus 4:10), but God used him to lead the Exodus and transmit 613 laws. Paul was the "chief" of all sinners (1 Timothy 1:15), a man who "made havoc of the church, entering every house, and dragging off men and women, committing them to prison" (Acts 8:3), but God made him into the most prolific apostle.

Throughout the Bible, God consistently bucks humanity's systems so that we can recognize His work and praise Him for it. When God uses us to achieve missions for His kingdom, the world sees His nature, not ours.

In the Gospel of Luke, a scholar tries to trick Jesus into contradicting the Hebrew Scriptures when he asks how one can attain eternal life. The scholar answers his own question by quoting Deuteronomy 6:5 and Leviticus 19:18: "'You shall love the Lord your

God with all your heart, with all your soul, with all your strength, and with all your mind,' and 'your neighbor as yourself'" (Luke 10:27).

And who is that "neighbor"? Jesus answers with a story:

> A certain man went down from Jerusalem to Jericho, and fell among thieves, who stripped him of his clothing, wounded him, and departed, leaving him half dead. Now by chance a certain priest came down that road. And when he saw him, he passed by on the other side. Likewise a Levite, when he arrived at the place, came and looked, and passed by on the other side. But a certain Samaritan, as he journeyed, came where he was. And when he saw him, he had compassion. So he went to him and bandaged his wounds, pouring on oil and wine; and he set him on his own animal, brought him to an inn, and took care of him. On the next day, when he departed, he took out two denarii, gave them to the innkeeper, and said to him, "Take care of him; and whatever more you spend, when I come again, I will repay you" (Luke 10:30-35).

The neighbor is the one "who had compassion" and "took care of him." Not the priest or Levite who were literal neighbors—presumably sharing the victim's Jewish faith and living in his community—but the Samaritan. He would have believed and worshipped and lived differently than the victim. Regardless of all his social differences, his actions made him the true neighbor.

WHO WERE THE SAMARITANS?

The Bible doesn't tell us a lot about this group of people, except that they worshipped the God of the Jews improperly, shared some familial history with the Jews, and were hated by their southern Jewish neighbors. You could say they were the ultimate underdogs.

In the New Testament, specifically, Jesus told His apostles not to go preach to the Samaritans but to focus on the Jews (Matthew 10:5-6); He did not stop in Samaria on His way to Jerusalem (Luke 9:52-53); only one in ten Samaritan lepers thanked Jesus for His healing (Luke 17:11-19); Jesus found hospitality there after debating theology with a promiscuous woman at a well (John 4); and finally, the Samaritans received the Holy Spirit after Philip, Peter, and John preached the gospel message and prayed over them (Acts 8:4-25). Take out their nationality, and that list could describe just about any group of Gentiles.

Historically we know a bit more. The Assyrian Empire, under the command of Sargon II, conquered the Northern Kingdom of Israel (which was also called Samaria, after its capital city) in 722 BCE. The Assyrians exported most if not all of the politically prominent Israelites from the Northern Kingdom and then imported refugees from other conquered areas of the empire. This was a common practice for ancient conquerors; a mixed population weakened the defeated nation and made future rebellion against the empire less likely. This had two major effects on the Northern Kingdom: the ten tribes of Israel that had made up the North were "lost," and the few Israelites who remained in Samaria intermarried with their new pagan neighbors.

After seven hundred years of multicultural blending, the people living in that region were known as the *Samaritans*. They believed in the Israelite God but could not worship Him in Jerusalem as He required in the law. Other pagan practices had slipped into their religion as well. This is why the Samaritan woman at the well said to Jesus, "Sir, it is obvious to me that You are a prophet. Our fathers worshiped here on this mountain, but Your people say that Jerusalem is the only place for all to worship. *Which is it?*" (John 4:19-20 THE VOICE). At that precise moment, Jerusalem was the location for the only temple where God resided. But that was about to change:

> The hour is coming when you will neither on this mountain, nor in Jerusalem, worship the Father. You worship what you do not know; we know what we worship, for salvation is of the Jews. But the hour is coming, and now is, when the true worshipers will worship the Father in spirit and truth; for the Father is seeking such to worship Him. God is Spirit, and those who worship Him must worship in spirit and truth (John 4:21-24).

Knowing His crucifixion and resurrection were imminent, Jesus answered her question in a way she may not have understood, but that future generations of readers certainly would.

Thankfully the church has many Samaritans (and in the twenty-first century, that moniker is no longer derogatory). I am thinking of the Sunday morning greeters, coffee makers, musicians, and sound technicians; those who serve in the nursery or teach Sunday school to children (and adults) of all ages; and those who clean the building and mow the lawn after the congregation has gone home for lunch. I am thinking of the everyday volunteers who tutor at-risk children, grab the mail for their elderly neighbors, give food to the homeless, and take care of aging loved ones. And I am thinking of those thoughtful enough to look up from their phones and greet a grocery cashier, hold open the door for a parent with a stroller, and slow down their car for a pedestrian in the crosswalk.

But can we Christians stop thinking so highly of ourselves and our own actions and opinions that we justify our disregard of those who don't think, act, or believe exactly as we do—or worse, that we justify attacking and hating others? Can we stop trying to change other people and open ourselves so the Holy Spirit can work to make us more like God? Can we realize that devoted churchgoers need God's grace just as much as those who have never before heard Jesus' name?

The Bible teaches that the world we now live in is not the perfect sin- and suffering-free garden He designed and wanted for us. Through Adam and Eve, we humans welcomed sin into His once-perfect creation, but thankfully God already had a plan that would reconcile us to Him. God sent His only Son, Jesus, to atone for the sins of all humanity; He then gave us the Bible so we can learn of Jesus' sacrifice, understand how He saved us, accept His gift of salvation, and tell the rest of the world about Him.

The Bible can be read from many different historical, textual, literary, and theological contexts, but the most important context is its religious context—its God context. Only the Holy Spirit can illuminate Scripture for Christians in the perfect way that God wants us to understand.

All Christians who consistently study God's Word will grow in their understanding of Him, so our opinions about Scripture and doctrine are likely to change over the years. In fact, they should change as we learn to better understand God and His Word. Knowing that what we believe today may be a theory we balk at and are tempted to mock tomorrow should encourage us to be humble and not prideful people.

May we be thankful that God loves us even when our beliefs, attitudes, and actions are wrong. He loved us as He created humanity,

He loved us when we were hiding behind His fig leaves in the garden, and He loved us when He sent His Son to die for us. Today He loves us as He disciplines us, and He loves us when we are worshipping Him through our studies, prayers, songs, and actions. For our God is not a God of tradition or doctrine; He's a God of love:

> Beloved, let us love one another, for love is of God; and everyone who loves is born of God and knows God. He who does not love does not know God, for God is love. In this the love of God was manifested toward us, that God has sent His only begotten Son into the world, that we might live through Him. In this is love, not that we loved God, but that He loved us and sent His Son to be the propitiation for our sins. Beloved, if God so loved us, we also ought to love one another (1 John 4:7-11).

Questions for Discussion and Reflection

1. Adam and Eve were the first but certainly not the only humans who desired all knowledge of good and evil so they could be like God. Today ignorance is seen as a shameful failing and not "bliss," as the saying goes. Are you afraid to say "I don't know"? Why or why not?

2. Each story, book, and Testament of the Bible highlights unique aspects of God's character that harmonize with other pieces to reveal Him to us. Based on what you have read in Scripture, how would you describe God to someone who doesn't know Him?

MANY THANKS TO...

...the staff and volunteers of Ashkelon's 2004 season—especially **Kate Birney**—who encouraged me to "not apologize for my good deeds" and taught me to trust my own judgment and abilities.

...my dearly loved **parents** and **siblings**, who never stopped believing I would write this book, listened to me stress as I did so, gave me ideas and edits, and supported my family by feeding David and walking Copper as I was hiding under my desk with a black-coffee IV and finishing this manuscript!

...my chosen sister **Melinda Phillips**, who jogged my memory at any hour of the day or night when I struggled to remember the details of lessons I'd learned or people I'd met at Harvard.

...**Lauren Brouhard** and **Lauren Stevens**, who kept me excited about writing and served as my first readers, editors, and advisors.

...my dear friend and future coauthor, **Stephanie Riggs**, whose collaboration led me to Harvest House and to publishing this book.

...my editor, **Kathleen Kerr**, who saw value in me and my writing just when I'd decided I was bankrupt. You revived my deep love of words, stories, and theology.

...**the team at Harvest House**, whose dedication to this project and enthusiasm for God's message have restored my faith in publishing.

...my dear husband and fellow basset-hound parent, **David Haley**, who for the last sixteen years has been my sidekick, confidant, and support staff. May we always agree on Clorox Wipes and Peanut Butter M&Ms, and may we never buy bologna again! I love you.

NOTES

Introduction

1. *Reading the Gospels with Gregory the Great: Homilies on the Gospels 21-26*, trans. Santha Bhattacharji (Petersham, MA: St. Bede's, 2001), 72.

2. Karen L. King, *The Gospel of Mary Magdala: Jesus and the First Woman Apostle* (Santa Rosa, CA: Polebridge, 2003), 5.5-6, 9.9.

Chapter 1: God's Library in One Book

1. Megan Sauter, "When Was Jesus Born—B.C. or A.D.? How the Divide Between B.C. and A.D. Was Calculated," *Bible History Daily*, November 29, 2017, https://www.biblicalarchaeology .org/daily/people-cultures-in-the-bible/jesus-historical-jesus/when-was-jesus-born-bc-or-ad/.

2. "Three Takes on the Oldest Hebrew Inscription," *Bible History Daily*, August 8, 2014, https:// www.biblicalarchaeology.org/scholars-study/three-takes-on-the-oldest-hebrew-inscription/.

3. Kathy Sawyer, "That Old Sheepskin Nowadays Probably Isn't-Baa," *Washington Post*, June 16, 1979, https://www.washingtonpost.com/archive/local/1979/06/16/that-old-sheepskin-nowadays -probably-isnt-baa/292864eb-0b9a-4b16-90c5-3954d2c8009a/?utm_term=.200bb1c42464.

4. Philip J. King and Lawrence E. Stager, *Life in Biblical Israel*, Library of Ancient Israel (Louisville, KY: Westminster John Knox, 2001), 162–64.

5. Rosalie David, *Handbook to Life in Ancient Egypt* (New York: Oxford University, 1999), 200.

6. Jeremy D. Smoak, "Words Unseen," *Biblical Archaeology Review* 44, no. 1 (2018): 52-59,70.

7. Oded Borowski, "Glossary: Tools of the Archaeological Trade," *Biblical Archaeology Review* 21, no. 1 (1995): 68-70, https://members.bib-arch.org/biblical-archaeology-review/13/5/4.

8. Sophie Ambler, "Stephen Langton," *Magna Carta Trust*, n.d., http://magnacarta800th.com /schools/biographies/magna-carta-bishops/stephen-langton/.

9. Bruce Metzger, *Manuscripts of the Greek Bible: An Introduction to Palaeography* (Oxford: Oxford University, 1981), 41.

10. "The Origins of the Red-Letter Bible," *Crossway*, March 23, 2006, https://www.crossway.org /articles/red-letter-origin/.

11. Ted Sorensen, *Counselor: A Life at the Edge of History* (New York: Harper Perennial, 2008), 146,151.

12. Brooke Hauser, "The Feminist Legacy of the Baby-Sitters Club," *New Yorker*, December 9, 2016, https://www.newyorker.com/books/page-turner/the-feminist-legacy-of-the-baby-sitters-club.

13. Nathaniel Hawthorne, *The Scarlet Letter* (1850; New York: Signet Classics, 2009), 193-94,258.

14. Michael W. Holmes, "To Be Continued…," *Bible Review* 17, no. 4 (2001): 12-14,16-23,48-49, https://members.bib-arch.org/bible-review/14/3/17.

15. Ibid.

Chapter 2: Don't Ignore Your Textbooks

1. *Cosmos: A Spacetime Odyssey*, featuring Neil deGrasse Tyson (Century City: 20th Century Fox, 2014), DVD, 553 minutes.

2. Joel Achenbach, "Why Carl Sagan Is Truly Irreplaceable: No One Will Ever Match His Talent as the 'Gatekeeper of Scientific Credibility,'" *Smithsonian Magazine*, March 2014, https://www.smithsonianmag.com/science-nature/why-carl-sagan-truly-irreplaceable-180949818/#xGIOeQXlqbtmsPPi.99.

3. Carl Sagan, *Cosmos: A Personal Journey*, episode 1, "The Shores of the Cosmic Ocean," aired September 28, 1980, on PBS.

4. Elizabeth Howell, "What Is the Big Bang Theory?" *Space.com*, November 7, 2017, https://www.space.com/25126-big-bang-theory.html.

5. Hanna Rosin, "Rock of Ages, Ages of Rock," *New York Times*, November 25, 2007, https://www.nytimes.com/2007/11/25/magazine/25wwln-geologists-t.html.

6. Carl Sagan, *Cosmos*, episode 1.

7. "How Does Carbon Dating Work?," *Beta Analytic Testing Laboratory*, https://www.radiocarbon.com/about-carbon-dating.htm.

8. Claude J. Allgre and Stephen H. Schneider, "Evolution of Earth," *Scientific American*, July 1, 2005, https://www.scientificamerican.com/article/evolution-of-earth/.

9. Angie Shumov, "Creation Myths from Around the World," *National Geographic*, n.d., http://channel.nationalgeographic.com/the-story-of-god-with-morgan-freeman/articles/creation-myths-from-around-the-world/.

10. Dave Itzkoff, "'Family Guy' Guy as Astrobiology Guy," *New York Times*, February 28, 2014, https://www.nytimes.com/2014/03/02/arts/television/seth-macfarlane-champions-new-cosmos-series-on-fox.html.

11. James M. Lundberg, "Thanks a Lot, Ken Burns: Because of You, My Civil War Lecture Is Always Packed," *Slate*, June 7, 2011, http://www.slate.com/articles/arts/culturebox/2011/06/thanks_a_lot_ken_burns.html.

12. Ronald S. Hendel, "The Search for Noah's Flood," *Bible History Daily*, March 27, 2014, https://www.biblicalarchaeology.org/daily/biblical-topics/hebrew-bible/the-search-for-noahs-flood/.

13. Michael D. Coogan, "In the Beginning: The Earliest History," in *The Oxford History of the Biblical World* (Oxford: Oxford University, 2001), 19-23.

14. Maureen Gallery Kovacs, trans., *The Epic of Gilgamesh* (Stanford: Stanford University, 1989), 101-02.

15. Biblical Archaeology Society, "The Exodus: Fact or Fiction? Evidence of Israel's Exodus from Egypt," *Bible History Daily*, March 28, 2018, https://www.biblicalarchaeology.org/daily/biblical-topics/exodus/exodus-fact-or-fiction/.

Chapter 3: George Washington Was No Cherry Picker

1. National Park Service, "History of the Cherry Trees," *Cherry Blossom Festival*, https://www.nps.gov/subjects/cherryblossom/history-of-the-cherry-trees.htm.

2. Mason Locke Weems, *The Life of Washington*, new ed., Peter S. Onuf, ed. (Armonk, New York and London: M.E. Sharpe), 8-10.

3. André Lemaire, "Education (Israel)," *Anchor Bible Dictionary*, 2:305-12.

4. J. Cheryl Exum, *Fragmented Women: Feminist (Sub)versions of Biblical Narratives* (Valley Forge, PA: Trinity, 1993), 176.

Chapter 4: Indiana Jones and the Buried Scriptures

1. "The Power of the Ark," *Indiana Jones and the Raiders of the Lost Ark*, directed by Steven Spielberg (1981; Los Angeles: Paramount, 2013), Blu-ray.

2. Joel Brinkley, "Archeologists Unearth 'Golden Calf' in Israel," *New York Times*, July 25, 1990, https://www.nytimes.com/1990/07/25/world/archeologists-unearth-golden-calf-in-israel .html.

3. Madeleine Mumcuoglu and Yosef Garfinkel, "The Puzzling Doorways of Solomon's Temple," *Biblical Archaeology Review* 41, no. 4 (2015): 35-41, https://members.bib-arch.org /biblical-archaeology-review/41/4/2.

4. Michael D. Danti, Darren P. Ashby, Marina Gabriel, and Susan Penacho, "Special Report: Current Status of the Tell Ain Dara Temple," *Bible History Daily*, March 9, 2018, https://www.biblicalarchaeology.org/daily/archaeology-today/cultural-heritage/special -report-current-status-tell-ain-dara-temple/.

5. Mary Joan Winn Leith, "From Seraph to Satan," *Bible Review* 20, no. 6 (2004): 6,46, https:// members.bib-arch.org/bible-review/20/6/2.

6. Trude Dothan, "Ekron of the Philistines, Part I: Where They Came From, How They Settled Down and the Place They Worshiped In," *Biblical Archaeology Review* 16, no. 1 (1990): 26-31,33-36, https://members.bib-arch.org/biblical-archaeology-review/16/1/2.

7. Casey Sharp, "Archaeological Views: Alternate Altars," *Biblical Archaeology Review* 41, no. 6 (2015): 28,78, https://members.bib-arch.org/biblical-archaeology-review/41/6/15.

8. Philip J. King and Lawrence E. Stager, *Life in Biblical Israel*, Library of Ancient Israel (Louisville, KY: Westminster John Knox, 2001), 234-36.

9. Ibid., 28-29.

10. Peter Schäfer, *The History of the Jews in Antiquity*, trans. David Chowcat (Luxembourg: Harwood Academic, 1995).

11. Anthony J. Saldarini, "Pharisees," *Anchor Bible Dictionary*, 5:298-303.

12. Gary G. Porton, "Sadducees," *Anchor Bible Dictionary*, 5:892-95.

13. Antiquities XVIII, 1.6 § 23 f.

14. Donald A. Hagner, *Matthew 1–13*, vol. 33A, *Word Biblical Commentary*, ed. Bruce Metzger et al. (Nashville: Word, 1993), 266.

Chapter 5: King Arthur's Many Authors

1. Michael Wood, "King Arthur, 'Once and Future King,'" *BBC History*, February 17, 2011, http:// www.bbc.co.uk/history/ancient/anglo_saxons/arthur_01.shtml.

2. Professor Schwartz wrote a paper about this exact topic: Baruch J. Schwartz, "What Really Happened at Mount Sinai?" *Bible Review* 13, no. 5 (1997): 20-30,46.

3. Richard Elliott Friedman, *Who Wrote the Bible?* (New York: HarperCollins, 1997), 236–37.

4. Stephen J. Patterson, "Q," *Bible Review* 9, no. 5 (1993): 34-41,61-62, https://members.bibarch .org/bible-review/9/5/18.

5. John S. Kloppenborg, *Q, the Earliest Gospel: An Introduction to the Original Stories and Sayings of Jesus* (Louisville, KY: Westminster John Knox, 2008), 125-27.

6. Steven Shisley, "Jesus and the Cross: How the Cross Became Christianity's Most Popular Symbol," *Bible History Daily*, March 26, 2018, https://www.biblicalarchaeology.org/daily/biblical-topics/crucifixion/jesus-and-the-cross/.

7. Bruce Metzger, *A Textual Commentary on the Greek New Testament*, 2nd ed. (Peabody, MA: Hendrickson Publishers, 2005), 123.

8. James Tabor, "The 'Strange' Ending of the Gospel of Mark and Why It Makes All the Difference," *Bible History Daily*, April 1, 2018, https://www.biblicalarchaeology.org/daily/biblical-topics/new-testament/the-strange-ending-of-the-gospel-of-mark-and-why-it-makes-all-the-difference/.

Chapter 6: Seeing Cinderella's Slipper Clearly

1. *Grimm's Complete Fairy Tales* (New York: Barnes and Noble, 1993), 84-85.

2. Graham Anderson, "The Cinderella Story in Antiquity," *Fairytale in the Ancient World* (New York: Routledge, 2000), 24-42.

3. "No Fairy Tale," *Ever After: A Cinderella Story*, directed by Andy Tennant (1998; Century City: 20th Century Fox, 1999), DVD.

4. Bernard F. Batto, "Red Sea or Reed Sea?" *Biblical Archaeology Review* 10, no. 4 (1984): 56-63, https://members.bib-arch.org/biblical-archaeology-review/10/4/3.

Chapter 7: Macbeth and the Self-Fulfilling Prophecies

1. "Welcome and Warning," *Harry Potter and the Prisoner of Azkaban*, directed by Alfonso Cuarón (Burbank: Warner Home Video, 2007), DVD.

2. *Macbeth*, ed. William Aldis Wright (London: Macmillian,1891), 4.1.10-11,18-19.

3. John J. Collins, ed. *Apocalypse: The Morphology of a Genre*, Semeia 14 (Missoula, MT: Society of Biblical Literature, 1979), 9.

4. F.F. Bruce, *1 and 2 Thessalonians*, vol. 45, *Word Biblical Commentary* (Dallas: Word, 1998), 127.

5. Jon Austin, "END OF THE WORLD? Has 'NASA Warned Planet X on a Straight Trajectory with Earth?'" *Express,* September 19, 2017, https://www.express.co.uk/news/weird/855616/End-of-the-World-The-Rapture-September-23-Nibiru-Planet-X-NASA.

6. Jamie Micklethwaite, "End of the World 2018: Bible Predicts 'Armageddon' THIS YEAR," *Daily Star*, January 2, 2018, https://www.dailystar.co.uk/news/latest-news/669724/end-of-world-2018-bible-armageddon-book-of-revelations-Mathieu-Jean-Marc-Joseph-Rodrigue.

Chapter 8: Too Many Cookbooks in the Christian Kitchen

1. David B. Barrett, George Thomas Kurian, Todd M. Johnson, *World Christian Encyclopedia: A Comparative Survey of Churches and Religions in The Modern World*, vol. 1, *The World by Countries: Religionists, Churches, Ministries* (Oxford: Oxford University, 2001), 14.

2. "John Calvin: Father of the Reformed Faith," *Christianity Today*, n.d., https://www.christianitytoday.com/history/people/theologians/john-calvin.html.

3. "Jacob Arminius: Irenic Anti-Calvinist," *Christianity Today*, n.d., https://www.christianitytoday.com/history/people/theologians/jacob-arminius.html.

4. "Evangelist Who Wants $54M Jet Says 'Jesus Wouldn't Be Riding a Donkey,'" CBS News, May 29, 2018, https://www.cbsnews.com/news/jesse-duplantis-evangelist-private-jet-jesus-wouldnt-be-riding-donkey-2018-05-29/.

5. Barrett, Kurian, and Johnson, *World Christian Encyclopedia*, 14.

6. Jaroslav Pelikan, *The Vindication of Tradition: 1983 Jefferson Lecture in the Humanities* (New Haven: Yale University Press, 1984), 65.

Chapter 9: The God Context

1. Daniel M. Master, "Giant of Iron Age Research: Lawrence E. Stager (1943–2017)," in "Remembering Three Giants," *Biblical Archaeology Review* 44, no. 4 (July/August 2018): 48-49.

2. John B. Dykes, "Holy, Holy, Holy," lyrics by Reginald Heber (1861; Hillsong, 2001).

ABOUT THE AUTHOR

Amanda Hope Haley holds a bachelor of arts in religious studies from Rhodes College and a master of theological studies in Hebrew Scripture and Interpretation from Harvard University.

She maintains a blog where she encourages women and men to challenge themselves to a deeper understanding of Scripture and to live whole lives in community with God, family, and each other. Her podcast, *The Red-Haired Archaeologist,* is also available on her website, http://www.amandahopehaley.com.

Amanda's first book, *Barren Among the Fruitful: Navigating Infertility with Hope, Wisdom, and Patience* was released by HarperCollins Christian Publishers in 2014 as part of the InScribed Collection. She contributed to The Voice Bible translation as a translator, writer, and editor; and she has been a content editor and ghostwriter for popular Christian authors.

Amanda and her husband, David, live in Chattanooga, Tennessee, with their always-entertaining basset hound, Copper.